Gallery Books
Editor: Peter Fallon

ARIEL

Marina Carr

ARIEL

Gallery Books

Ariel
is first published
simultaneously in paperback
and in a clothbound edition
on the day of its première,
2 October 2002.

The Gallery Press
Loughcrew
Oldcastle
County Meath
Ireland

© Marina Carr 2002

ISBN 1 85235 331 7 (*paperback*)
    1 85235 332 5 (*clothbound*)

A CIP catalogue record for this book
is available from the British Library.

All rights whatsoever in this play are strictly reserved. Application for performance in any medium or for translation into any language should be addressed to the author's sole agent c/o Leah Schmidt, The Agency (London) Ltd, 24 Pottery Lane, Holland Park, London W11 4LZ, England.

The Gallery Press acknowledges the financial assistance of An Chomhairle Ealaíon / The Arts Council, Ireland, and the Arts Council of Northern Ireland.

Characters

FERMOY FITZGERALD
FRANCES FITZGERALD, *his wife*
ARIEL FITZGERALD, *their daughter*
ELAINE FITZGERALD, *child of twelve and young woman*
STEPHEN FITZGERALD, *child of ten and young man*
BONIFACE, *monk, Fermoy's older brother*
SARAH, *aunt of Fermoy*
HANNAFIN
VERONA, *interviewer*
SOUNDMAN/WOMAN
CAMERAMAN/WOMAN

Time and place

Act One, the present
Act Two, ten years later
Act Three, two months later

Dining room of the Fitzgerald home (table, drinks cabinet, CD player, chairs, two entrances)

Music

Theme music: 'Mors et Vita' from Gounod's *Judex*.

Ariel was first produced in the Abbey Theatre, in association with Fiach MacConghail, on Wednesday, 2 October 2002, with the following cast:

FERMOY	Mark Lambert
ELAINE	Eileen Walsh
SARAH	Joan O'Hara
HANNAFIN	Des Cave
BONIFACE	Barry McGovern
FRANCES	Ingrid Craigie
ARIEL	Elske Rahill
STEPHEN	Dylan Tighe
VERONA	Caitríona Ní Mhurchú
YOUNG STEPHEN	Paul McGovern
	Shane Murray Corcoran
YOUNG ELAINE	Siobhán Cullen
	Lydia Rahill

Director	Conall Morrison
Set Design	Frank Conway
Costume Design	Joan O'Clery
Lighting Design	Rupert Murray
Fight Director	Renny Krupinski
Stage Director	Audrey Hession
ASM	Maree Kearns

for Dermot, William and Daniel

ACT ONE

Curtain up. Lights up as FERMOY, FRANCES, ARIEL, ELAINE, BONIFACE, STEPHEN *and* SARAH *stand around a birthday cake on the table. The cake is lit with sixteen candles. All are singing:*

ALL 'And so say all of us,
And so say all of us,
For she's a jolly good fella,
For she's a jolly good fella,
For she's a jolly good fella,
And so say all of us.'

> ARIEL *blows out the candles, claps and cheers.*

FRANCES Happy birthday, sweetheart. (*Kisses her*)
BONIFACE Sweet sixteen and never been kissed. (*Kisses her*)
FERMOY We hope, we have our doubts.
ARIEL What ya don't know won't bother ya. Does this mane I get the keys a the car, Daddy?
FERMOY Mebbe ud manes ya get your own little banger.
ARIEL Whah?
FERMOY Look ouh the winda.

> ARIEL *runs to window followed by* ELAINE.

ARIEL Ah, Daddy, you're mad, you're mad.

> FERMOY *gives her the keys, lifts her up, sings to her, dancing around the room.*

FERMOY 'Whin first I seen the love ligh in your eye
I thought the world held nough buh jiy for me
And aven though we drifted far apart
I love ya as I loved ya,
Whin ya were sweet, whin ya were sweet sixteen.'

(*Puts her down*) You're noh a child anymore buh we'll hould onta ya long as we can, won't we, Frances?

FRANCES Leh go, Stephen, leh go a me dress. (*To* FERMOY) Yeah, a cuurse we will.

ARIEL Can I go drivin now?

FERMOY Were ya drinkin wine?

ARIEL Just a glass.

FRANCES Yeah, come an, I'll go for a spin wud ya.

Exit ARIEL, FRANCES, STEPHEN.

SARAH Anywan for cake?

FRANCES When we come back.

SARAH (*Exiting, muttering to herself*) Was up half the nigh makin thah. Whin I was a girl we had wan cake ah Christmas, now ud's cake all the time, cake and more cake, swear ud was Versailles yees were brough up in.

FERMOY Elaine, g'wan wud your mother, good girl.

ELAINE Sing a song to me, Daddy, sing sweet sixteen to me.

FERMOY Whin you're sweet sixteen, darlin, then I'll sing sweet sixteen to you.

ELAINE Sure thah's years away.

FERMOY Ah g'wan for a drive in Ariel's new car, good girl.

ELAINE Will ya gimme a puff a your cigar if I go?

FERMOY Whin ya come back I'll give ya a puff.

ELAINE And a swig a brandy?

FERMOY Two puffs and two swigs if ya lave me in peace for five minutes.

ELAINE Alrigh so. I'll be back shortly to hould ya to your word.

Exit ELAINE.

FERMOY I've no doubt ya will. God, they'd drive ya mad, kids. I spind the whole day duckin them.

BONIFACE And me thinkin ya were an adorin father.

FERMOY And I am, an adorin father who doesn't know what

to do wud em. I can't waih for Mondays. Wakinds should be banned. More paple gets murdered on Sundays than any other day a the wake. Whah does thah mane?

BONIFACE I suppose ud's wan way a passin the time after the roast beef and the trifle.

FERMOY (*Pouring brandy for himself*) Ya still on the wagon?

BONIFACE Liver like a newborn. For whah, I ask meself.

FERMOY (*Pouring a coke for* BONIFACE) And how's things up ah the monastery?

BONIFACE The last a the Mohicans. I'm the ony wan under sixty. Spind me days changin nappies, ferryin thim to hospitals, funeral parlours, checkin they take their medication, givin em glasses a whiskey to shuh em up, breakin up fights over armchairs and toffees. They go ah wan another like three-year-aulds. Caugh Celestius goin for the back of Aquinus' head wud a hommer last wake. I swiped ud ouh a hees hand just in the nick a time. Noh today, I says to Celestius, noh today, and he gives me this avil grin and slinks off. And Aquinus manewhile is oblivious to the whole thing, he's dribblin and droolin away to hees horse. He has this horse goes everywhere wud him.

FERMOY Noh a rale horse?

BONIFACE No, no, ud's all in hees addled little head. Him and the horse does everthin together, makes room in the bed for him and all. There's a place seh for him ah the table, betwane me and Aquinus. No wan else'll sih beside the horse. Ya'd want to see Aquinus fadin him rashers. I don't enquire whah goes on in bed betwane em. I'm afraid he'd tell me. And Bonaventura is in intensive care, thanks be to the lord God.

FERMOY He's the wan calls ya Mammy?

BONIFACE Thah's him. And whin he's lucid he's worse. Wint inta see him yesterda, gev him a Padre Pio relic and he flings ud back ah me. Whah do I want wud Padre Pio's britches, says he. Well, is there anhin I

13

can get ya, says I. There is, he says, me youh and Billie Holida. And then he goes into a swirl abouh bein cremahed, thah he's noh a Catholic anymore, thah he never belaved in the first place, and him takin chunks ouha the chalice hees whole life. And despihe all the lunacy they cry like babbies at nigh, hare em whingin in their cells. Some part of em knows ud's over and they goh ud all wrong and still they hang on.

FERMOY Well, wouldn't you?

BONIFACE Apparently I am. Are ya goin to swing ud this time?

FERMOY Ud'll be a dogfigh.

BONIFACE Aye, Hannafin's mug is everywhere, he's some cowbiy, had the nerve to come canvassin me ah the monastery.

FERMOY Whah had he to say for heeself?

BONIFACE Asked me to talk sinse to you. Tould me to tell ya ya don't stand a chance, that you're ony makin a fool a yourself.

FERMOY Four votes. Four. That's all was in ud last time.

BONIFACE He still has the whole machine behind him. You're on your own.

FERMOY I've God behind me and what's a little civil war coven compared to God backin ya. I'll geh in this time alrigh. Been havin powerful drames lately. Drames of a conqueror.

BONIFACE Have ya now?

FERMOY Oh, aye. Dreamt last nigh I was dinin wud Alexander the Greah, Napoleon and Caesar, and we all had tigers' feeh under the whihe linen tablecloth. Ud was brillint. And ya know thah famous portrait a Napoleon, up on hees whihe horse, the fah legs of him diggin inta the flanks, off to destriy the world? Well, I can't stop dramin abouh thah picture, ony I'm the wan on the whihe horse insteada Napoleon.

BONIFACE Noh another wan wud a horse. You should take up wud Aquinus.

FERMOY Laugh away. Me and God's on a wan to wan.

BONIFACE Oh, excuse me. And whin did this greah event occur?

Ud wasn't in the papers.

FERMOY Ya think I'm jokin. I'm tellin ya I've direct access to him.

BONIFACE Well, you're the first I meh thah has. Tell him to scahher a few bars a gold in my pah next time yees are houldin hands.

FERMOY The last person ya should ever talk to abouh God is wan a the religious. Yees are the most cynical, rational, mathemahical shower I ever cem across whin ud comes to God.

BONIFACE Ya have to be mathemahical when you're dalin wud mystery.

FERMOY Well, yees have him ruined for all true belavers.

BONIFACE What do ya expect? Facts are he hasn't been seen for over two thousand year, for all we know he's left the solar system. We're goin on hearsay, gossip, the buuk. Times I wonder was he ever here.

FERMOY Well, if he wasn't none of ud makes sinse.

BONIFACE There's many belaves wasn't him med the earth ah all, thah ud was Satan and hees fallen armies, thah we were masterminded in hell, only Lucifer's pawns to geh ah God. Now I wouldn't go thah far meself, ih'd be too frightenin if thah was the case, buh for you to claim the privelege a God's ear is ouhrageous. Ud's blasphemy. Does paple belave in blasphemy anymore?

FERMOY I do.

BONIFACE Well, if ya do why're ya claimin God's talkin to ya?

FERMOY I'm claimin natin, forget the whole thing.

BONIFACE No, ya've me curious now. And whah does he say to ya?

FERMOY I'm noh tellin ya, forgeh ud, cheers. (*Raises his glass, drinks*)

BONIFACE I've offindid ya.

FERMOY I'm sick a ya talkin down to me from the heights a your canon law and the foosterins a the Pope a Rome and your cosy mehaphysics and your charihy. For all your religion ya know natin abouh the nature a God.

BONIFACE And you do?

FERMOY I know a couple a things.

BONIFACE And tell me, what's he like, this God a yours?

FERMOY Oh, he's beauhiful. When he throws hees head back hees hair gets tangled in the stars, and in hees hands are seven moons thah he juggles like worry beads. Hees eyes is shards of obsidian, hees skin is turquoise, and hees mouth is a staggerin red, whah the first red musta been before ud all started fadin. I'm noh capturin him righ, for how can ya parse whah is perfect.

BONIFACE My God is an auld fella in a tent, addicted to broccoli.

FERMOY No, God is young. He's so young. He's on fire for us, heaven reelin wud hees rage at not bein among us, the eternihy of eternihy hauntin him. Time manes natin to him. He rises from an afternoon nap and twinty centuries has passed.

BONIFACE No, no, no, he never slapes. Christianihy is based on God never slapin. You're wrong there, God does noh slape.

FERMOY My God slapes.

BONIFACE How d'ya know, did ya tuck him in? Rade him a bedtime story?

FERMOY Didn't I see him, a mountain slapin on a mountain.

BONIFACE Ah, you've had too much brandy.

FERMOY Don't you try pullin rank wud me, wud your cross and your robes and your broccoli God. I entered the landscape a God before you, long before. You can't tell me anhin abouh God.

BONIFACE Ya talkin abouh Ma, a'ya?

FERMOY No, I'm noh talkin abouh Ma. Why d'ya have to brin her up every time?

BONIFACE Do I brin her up every time?

FERMOY Wudouh fail.

BONIFACE And is thah a crime?

FERMOY Was thirty-five year ago, Boniface. She's gone, she's gone.

BONIFACE And whah an exih.

FERMOY She was never the suurt was goin to die in her bed.

BONIFACE She'd a died in her bed if she'd been leh . . . I remember goin home to see you wan time, soon after, and Auntie Sarah was sittin ah the table wearin Ma's clothes, the hair up in wan of her slides, prancin round the kitchen like ud was hers.

FERMOY Someone had to wash the dishes.

BONIFACE Now ud's comin ouh.

FERMOY Whah?

BONIFACE Thah I didn't lave the novitiate to look after ya.

FERMOY Auntie Sarah looked after me fine, fierce good to me, a packet a biscuits and a bottle a red lemonade every nigh before I wint to bed, whah more could ya ask for?

BONIFACE A wonder ya've a tooth in your head. No, shoulda been me looked after ya, ony I was a maniac for religion ah the time. I goh the full benefih a Ma's christianihy, no douh abouh thah, a novice ah seventeen. Ya know ud never occurred to me to go agin her. At laste ya were spared thah, buh I shoulda looked after ya.

FERMOY I grew up, didn't I? Furthest thing from me mind righ now. I've an election to win. D'you think I stand a chance?

BONIFACE Hannafin has the core vohe. He's held thah seat for twinty year. Be hard budge him.

FERMOY Nearly done ud last time. This time I will.

BONIFACE Whah makes ya so sure?

FERMOY Horse sinse and God. That's all ya nade to get by in this world, horse sinse and God. That's whah goh me this far and thah's what'll take me to the moon.

BONIFACE Ya may geh past Hannafin first.

FERMOY Ah, ud's noh Hannafin's the crux ah all, ud's meself, allas meself. Hannafin's a gombeen, like the rest of em. Why do they all want to be nice? What's so greah abouh bein liked? Am I missin somethin here? Swear ud was beahification they were after and em all cut-throats in their own kitchens. All chirpin the wan tune like there's no other — aqual wages, crèches in the workplace, no ceilin on the women, the pace process, a leg up for the poor, the handicapped, the refugees, the tinkers, the tachers, the candlestick makers. In Sparta they were left on the side a the hill and that's where I'll lave em when I've the reins. I swear to God I'm goin to brin in a new religion, no more guilt, no more sorrow, no more good girls and good biys, just the unstoppable blood pah a the soul.

BONIFACE Ya wont win an election on thah speech.

FERMOY Migh surprise ya to know how many agrays wud me. The earth's over, paple knows thah in their bones, ozone layer in tahhers, oceans gone to sewer, whole world wan big landfill a dirty nappies. We're goin to lave this place in ashes like the shower on Mars.

BONIFACE I don't belave in much anymore. Gardenin, if ud was puh to me and me back to the wall I'd say I belave in cornflowers. I'd like to think whahever happens us thah this ground will survive us.

FERMOY The age a cornflowers is dead and gone. Last two thousand year a complahe farce. Well, ud's nearly over. We'll pick up where we left off.

BONIFACE And where's thah?

FERMOY The mortal sins is back in fashion. Welcome back, we missed yees. Age a compassion had uds turn, never took rooh. Well, way past time to banish the dregs to heaven's dungeon. The earth is ours wance more and noh before time.

BONIFACE If thah's your manifesto I may start prayin ya don't geh in.

FERMOY Ud's mine for the takin, I know ud is, all ud nades on my part is a sacrifice.

BONIFACE Whah suurt of a sacrifice?

FERMOY A sacrifice to God.

BONIFACE Buh whah suurt?

FERMOY The only suurt he acknowledges. Blood.

BONIFACE Blood?

FERMOY This thing's been edgin me to the cliff all year. And there's more. If I don't offer up this sacrifice he demands, he's goin to take ud anyway. And me for good measure. Whichever road I take is crooked. Thah's the price a God. If I make the sacrifice, then ud's all mine. Buh the cost, the cost. Impossible. Buh if I refuse this sacrifice, I'm facin the grave meself and, worse, facin him after refusin me destiny and, worse agin, after refusin him the wan thing he asks as payment for this enchanted life.

BONIFACE Spakin a blood, ours is streaked, Fermoy. You know thah well as me. The auld fella.

FERMOY This is different. We're talkin a different league here. We're talkin whah I was puh on this earth for.

BONIFACE Nowan knows whah they're on the earth for.

FERMOY I do. I'm on this earth to rule. Was born knowin ud. Timidihy has held me back till now. Ud'll hould me back no longer. I refuse to spind any more a me life on the margins. I refuse to succumb to an early exih. I'll give him whah he wants for ud's hees in the first place anyway.

BONIFACE And whah is ud he wants?

FERMOY I tould ya, blood and more blood, blood till we're dry as husks, then pound us down, spread us like salt on the land, begin the experiment over, on different terms next time.

BONIFACE We've moved beyond the God a Job, Fermoy. Two thousand year a civilization has taken us to a different place. Now I'm noh sayin this is Utopia or anywhere near ud, buh we have advanced a few small steps along the way. And for you to call up the auld God is terrifyin. I don't care how beauhiful he appears. He's a wolf and ud's a wolf you'll be growlin wud if ya dredge him up. You're playin dangerous games here. God does noh do dales, ah laste the God I know doesn't. I mane whah exactly is this blood sacrifice? Is ud some suurt a pagan calf ritual or are we talkin somethin far older and more sinister here?

FERMOY Can't a man air the festerins of hees soul withouh bein convicted?

BONIFACE No, I don't think he can. Thah's why there's such a thing as custody a the tongue. Thah's why our thoughts is silent, so we can do away wud em before they're spoken. And ud's a mighy short journey from sayin a thing to doin ud.

FERMOY Ah, forget the whole bleddy business.

BONIFACE Ih'd fit yourself behher to forgeh ud.

FERMOY Alrigh. Alrigh. Ud's forgotten. Gone. I'll lave ud wud the nigh where ud belongs and hope ud'll lave me. In the manetime I've an election comin and I've a problem wud the hospitals, wonderin could ya help me.

BONIFACE If I can.

FERMOY Ud's all the wans dyin in their beds wud their faces to the wall, nade their votes.

BONIFACE Ah, would ya lave em alone.

FERMOY Ya think I want to be botherin thim? There's only a spider's leg between me and Hannafin. Whah would ya say to a dyin person thah'd make em vote for ya?

BONIFACE Say natin ony sih and talk to em.

FERMOY I'm noh the Sisters a Mercy, talk to em abouh whah?

BONIFACE I'd'n know . . . heaven, mebbe?

FERMOY Whah? Say natin abouh votin ony soother em wud eternihy? Alrigh, I've a good workin knowledge of eternihy. I'll melt em wud pictures of uds silver avenues and uds houses a tarnished gold and the blue waher lappin offa the whihe marble pier as the brass-bodied angels grates em wud mugs a tay. If they don't serve tay in heaven there won't be an Irish person in the place.

BONIFACE And ya call yourself religious.

FERMOY Yes, I do, buh my eternihy is noh for the herd.

BONIFACE The herd's eternihy will do fine for me.

FERMOY No douh ud will, a swate little postcard heaven. Have you any idea of the vastness of heaven? Your heaven would fih on a stamp. Mine can noh be measured.

BONIFACE Then I think ud's a dangerous thing noh to have the square rooh a heaven in your mind.

FERMOY Look, I nade to wrihe a lehher to thah eegih thah
runs the health buurd. Whah's this hees name is
agin? The wan wud the coconuh hair?

BONIFACE Alloni.

FERMOY Thah's him, noh returnin me calls. I nade the run a
the hospitals, auld folks homes, day cintres, thah
suurt a thing. You should know the kind a lehher
thah'll geh him. He's givin Hannafin free rein and
he won't leh me in. What's hees pisin anyway?

BONIFACE Bates the wife. Mebbe he's stopped. See her goin
round wudouh her sunglasses, perfect face on her.

FERMOY Anhin else?

BONIFACE He puh wan a hees kids in hospital a while back.
Med em take ouh her appendix, noh a thing wrong
a the girl.

FERMOY I suppose if ya run the health buurd ya can have
the whole family operahed on for free.

BONIFACE Mebbe ud was a sign of affection.

FERMOY Or a birthday present. Come an down to the den
and we shape this lehher. (*Upwards*) I'll geh in yet,
sir, wud or wudout ya. (*Exiting by the cake*) Ya want
a slice a cake?

BONIFACE Naw.

FERMOY Me aither. Hate cake, so does the kids.

He smashes the cake.

Allas wanted to do thah to a cake. Ah, Auntie
Sarah, spyin agin.

SARAH Wanta be fierce bored to be perchin on your
conversation. I hear Hannafin's goin to win.

FERMOY Ya won't rise me, missus.

SARAH Only tellin ya the word abroad.

FERMOY I won't be countin on your vohe so.

SARAH And the missus is votin green, heard her on the
phone.

FERMOY Ah, the little protest vohe. The Granes'll comes
back to me ivintually. She'll vohe for me in spihe of
herself. Why does all the women in this house

want to kill me?

SARAH Law a the world, don't take ud personally.

Exit BONIFACE *and* FERMOY *as* ARIEL *enters, talking on her mobile.* SARAH *tries to fix the cake.*

ARIEL (*On her mobile*) Yeah, a suurt of a buhherfly yella . . . brand new, I swear . . . Yeah . . . Whah're y'up to? . . . Yeah, I seen ud, fierce, isn't ud? . . . Ya love ud? Ah, ud's wocious, ya still belave in Noddyland, ah, Stephanie . . . Yeah, yeah, whah time yees matin ah? . . . No, they'll never leh me, never leh me anywhere, afraid somewan'd run off wud me. I wish . . . Did he say he'd be there? . . . Damn ud . . . Sunda nigh they'll never leh me . . .

FRANCES (*Entering*) You're goin nowhere in the dark, Ariel, so don't bother askin.

ARIEL (*Exiting*) Ah, Ma . . . (*To Stephanie on the mobile*) Ya heard thah, did ya? Look, tell him I'll see him in school tomorra . . . Yeah, yeah. (*She's well offstage by now*)

FRANCES Whah happened the cake?

SARAH Didn't heeself puh hees fist through ud.

FRANCES (*To* STEPHEN *who stands beside her, looking at her*) I said no, Stephen, you're noh getting ud.

STEPHEN Just a sup.

FRANCES I'm noh a lollypop.

STEPHEN (*Climbing on her knee*) Come an and don't be so manchey wud em. (*Going for her breast*)

FRANCES I said, no. (*Stops him*) No, Stephen, no. (*A struggle*)

SARAH Ah, leh him suck away. If there was wan goin I'd be suckin on ud too.

FRANCES (*Struggling with him*) No way, Stephen. Whah would your Daddy say?

STEPHEN Don't you dare tell him!

FRANCES I'll tell him righ now if ya don't stop.

STEPHEN Alrigh, alrigh, just leh me lie up agin ya. (*Lies up against her*)

FRANCES Don't fall aslape on me now, I'm warnin ya. (*To*

SARAH) Here, give us a bih a cake, love cake, I'd ahe ud all down to the plahe.

SARAH *gives her a lump of cake. Enter* ELAINE.

Ya want a bih a cake, Elaine?

ELAINE No. (*Stands there watching* FRANCES)

FRANCES Damn ud, he's aslape.

ELAINE He's ony pretendin.

FRANCES Wake up, Stephen, come an wake up, love. (*To* ELAINE) What do ya want, peh?

ELAINE Natin, just lookin at ya.

FRANCES Did ya like Ariel's birthday?

ELAINE No.

FRANCES And why, migh I ask?

ELAINE Birthdays is ony interestin when they're your own.

FRANCES A'ya lookin for a scrap, are ya?

ELAINE Yeah, I am.

FRANCES Ya'd too much coke, that's what's wrong a ya.

ELAINE Daddy tould ya noh to be doin thah thing wud Stephen.

FRANCES Whah thing? I'm noh doin anhin wud him.

ELAINE You're a liar. A big liar.

FRANCES Don't you call me a liar, and stop givin me the avil eye. I'm tired, Elaine, I'm tired.

ELAINE *stands there looking at* FRANCES.

SARAH She's like her grandmother, thah wan, she'd stare the world down, biggest eyes y'ever seen. I goh the hands, she goh the eyes.

ELAINE And where is me grandmother?

SARAH Never you mind where she is.

ELAINE She's ah the bohhom a Cuura Lake where me grandaddy puh her, in a bag wud a boulder, nowan ever found her.

FRANCES If ya know why're ya askin?

ELAINE Want to hear her say ud. She's ah the bohhom a Cuura Lake where me grandaddy puh her. Love the sound a thah.

SARAH   Ya do, don't ya, ya babby witch in the cauldron. Thah child knows too much.

ELAINE   And where were you when ud was happenin, Auntie Sarah?

SARAH   Never you mind where I was.

ELAINE   Ya were warmin me grandaddy's bed, that's where ya were.

SARAH   And what's ud to you if I was?

ELAINE   Ud's information and information is useful.

FRANCES   Thah's enough, Elaine. G'wan ouhside the duur and don't come back in till ya say sorry to Auntie Sarah.

ELAINE   Well, ud's true, isn't ud, what's to be sorry for when ud's true? (*Squeezes* FRANCES)

FRANCES   Ow, ya rip, ya!

ELAINE   Thah's for the last twelve years.

FRANCES   Geh ouh!

ELAINE   (*Sauntering out*) Ya think ud bothers me goin ouhside the duur? Love ud ouh there. Can't waih to be ouhside your duur forever.

SARAH   There's a madam. I'd like to see her whin she's twinty-wan.

FRANCES   Thah child hates me, I don't know why ud is, buh thah child hates me.

SARAH   Mebbe she'll grow ouh of ud.

FRANCES   Ud's noh natural. From the very beginnin she wanted rid a me. Times I think she's me penance for James. Isn't thah an awful thing to think?

SARAH   High time you stopped torturin yourself over James.

FRANCES   Why will no wan in this house leh me talk abouh James? Fermoy goes mad if I mention him, he thinks I'm blamin him. If I wanted to I could, for James' death was as much hees fault as mine. I wanted to brin him on the honeymoon. Fermoy says no, lave him wud your aunts. And oh . . . when they rang and tould me . . . three thousand miles away and James dead from the belt of a hurl . . . still can't belave ud. (*Produces locket*) Look ah him. And hees father. I wasn't good to thah man. Two calves they were. Look at them.

SARAH Seen ud before, Frances, seen ud before, many, many times.

FRANCES Aye . . . and these tears is natin to the wans I'll shed in the future. I still have to pay for James. Every mornin I ask meself is this the day the roof's goin to fall in for whah I done to James. And if I as much as look ouh the winda a second too long or pause in the hall of an avenin, Fermoy goes inta a reel of how I loved James and the first husband more than him. Well mebbe I did. Fermoy threw the dust in me eyes. These two I loved.

SARAH (*Exiting with dishes*) The beauhiful dead, the beauhiful dead, everywan loves em.

ELAINE (*Head around the door*) I've a fierce destiny, Ma, and you're in ud.

SARAH (*Shoos her out*) Away wud ya and lave your mother alone.

FRANCES *sits there with* STEPHEN *asleep on her knee, looking at locket. She looks from locket to* STEPHEN *to locket. She strokes his head.*

FRANCES You've a look of him alrigh. The eyes, yees boh have my eyes. Buh ya don't have hees black curls, you've Fermoy's hair. James had the most beauhiful, beauhiful head a blue black curls. Paple'd stop us in the street to touch hees curls. I had to puh a clip in your hair to kape the curls ouha your eyes and still I wouldn't cuh em. Whin a'ya goin to cuh thah child's hair, they'd ask. Never, I'd say, never, and I never did. Five years a black curls wint inta thah grave and me wud em.

Enter BONIFACE.

BONIFACE I'm away, Frances. Ah, the child, the child, is there anhin lovelier than a slapin child?

FRANCES There is, aye. A dead wan. (*Closes locket*)

BONIFACE Is thah so?

FRANCES If he doesn't geh in this time there'll be war.

BONIFACE He's overdue a dressin down.

FRANCES Help him, will ya, Boniface? He's us all driven mad here, you know everywan, geh em to vohe for him. He's noh a bad man, just all wrong, behher than Hannafin.

BONIFACE Ah, Hannafin's harmless, he's the auld school, sell the whole country down the Swanee for an extension to hees bungalow and a new jape.

FRANCES Well, I'm the wan'll suffer if he doesn't geh in. I'm the wan'll be blemt.

BONIFACE I've an awful falin he's goin to swing ud. He's down there in the den rattlin on abouh blood sacrifice and destiny and vision. God help us all if he gets in, thah's whah I say. The auld fella was a tyrant too.

FRANCES I ony meh him the wance, thought he was a fine auld gintleman.

BONIFACE He'd the charm a forty divils alrigh. They allas do, buh back a the charm was the stuck-up rebellis heart of all a Lucifer's crew. Does he ever talk to ya abouh the auld lad?

FRANCES Me and thah man doesn't talk ah all. Wance ya go past hello wud Fermoy he wants to kill ya. Asier say natin.

BONIFACE Ask him abouh the auld lad and Ma sometime.

FRANCES God, no, don't want to open thah buuk a butchery. Sooner leh an ud never happened.

BONIFACE Oh, ud happened, and me man in there in the middle of ud all. Auld fella med him hould Ma down.

FRANCES He was ony a child, wasn't he, wasn't hees fault.

BONIFACE I'm noh sayin ud was. All I'm sayin is somethin like thah is bound to take uds toll on a person's view a the world. I don't like the way he's goin an.

FRANCES And why did your father do ud?

BONIFACE In cuurt he said ud was to save her the trouble a dyin laher an. Figure thah wan ouh at your leisure.

FRANCES And whah had she done? I don't mane she deserved

to be puh in a bag and pegged to the bohhom of a lake, buh whah was goin an?

BONIFACE He tried to make ouh she was havin an affair. She wasn't. Thah woman was in love wud wan man and wan man only. Padre Pio of San Giovanni.

FRANCES Hard compate wud Padre Pio.

BONIFACE Her party piece was Padre Pio hearin her confession. And ah the end of ud he puh hees hand through the curtain and the stigmaha bled onta her blouse. She had the blouse folded in tissue paper wud lavender sprigs all over ud. And if ya were really good she'd take down the blouse and leh us trace our fingers over the blood. That's eternihy you're touchin, she'd say. That's eternihy, be careful wud ud. Christ, I could tell ya stories abouh thah woman, never a dull moment, and the eyelashes on her and the big dark mane of her, like a horse, like a beauhiful Egyptian horse. And the auld lad doesn't know whah to do wud her so he does away wud her.

FRANCES And Fermoy there in the middle of ud all. The size a the nigh in thah man is past measurin.

FERMOY *has entered.*

FERMOY Is ud now? . . . Was he on ya agin?

FRANCES He's ony sittin on me knee.

FERMOY Know you're lyin. Can smell the milk.

FRANCES You slape better ah nigh thinkin I'm a liar.

FERMOY I certainly do. (*Takes* STEPHEN) C'mere, me little man, till we snake some gristle inta your drames.

FRANCES Whah'd ya go and mash the cake for? Ya know I love cake.

FERMOY And ya love witholdin ud. I'm married to a nun, Boniface, a born agin virgin. Ud's noh every man can say he's hitched hees cart to the reverend mother.

BONIFACE Ya may lave me ouha the sheets.

FRANCES I'll take off me wimple when you learn how to

trahe a woman righ and noh before.

FERMOY And where am I supposed to learn? On a rockin horse?

FRANCES Ya know natin, Fermoy Fitzgerald.

FERMOY Then tell me, missus! G'wan, tell me! Listen to this now, Boniface, listen to wan of her dirges on love.

FRANCES Waste a breah dirgin you.

FERMOY Sure, the only rason I married ya was so I could have ud on demand. And all she does is talk abouh ud, talk abouh ud wud this lad here latched onto her. Look ah hees teeth, he's whah? Ten, and he still has hees milk teeth. They won't fall ouh till she weans him. Buh she won't wean him. Ya know why? Because then she'd have to dale wud me. I've the length a you, missus. I know whah's goin on in thah little bantam head a yours. You should be tratin me like a king steada grindin me down to bone male.

FRANCES You and your auld election. Ya never have a nice word. Ya never have a word. (*Exiting*) In and ouh like a fox. Sooner be palin a bag a spuds.

FERMOY (*Goes after her, yanks locket from her neck*) Knew ud! Just knew ud. Sure there's no talkin to ya when ya've thah yoke round your neck.

FRANCES Gimme thah back if ya value your life.

FERMOY (*Fending her off*) Look whah she wears round her neck.

FRANCES Give us ud.

BONIFACE Ah, would ya give the woman her locket.

FERMOY Look ah him! Look whah I have to puh up wud. The first husband. Pugnacious puss of him.

FRANCES Gimme thah back now, ya gone too far.

FERMOY High time ya forgoh abouh them. They're dead. Dead as stones. I'm your husband. There's your son (*Stephen*).

FRANCES (*Pointing at locket*) And there's me other son. Look ah him if ya dare. The wan ya killed.

FERMOY Oh, here we go.

FRANCES You killed him or as good as.

FERMOY How, tell me how did I kill him and I on another continent?

FRANCES Wud black thinkin and wishin him away.

FERMOY Brin him wud us, I told ya. Brin him on the bleddy honeymoon for all I care.

FRANCES Like hell ya said brin him wud us. You're greah ah re-jiggin the past, allas wud yourself as the haroh. Give him to me, ud's me favourihe picture, give him to me.

FERMOY Well now, missus, you shoulda taken the edge off of me this morning.

Exit FERMOY.

BONIFACE Y'alrigh?

FERMOY This is ony the warm up. This is natin.

BONIFACE Ya want me to get your locket back?

FRANCES No, thah's whah he'd like. Leh him cool hees jets. He'll be back for another round.

BONIFACE Righ, I'm away durin the calm.

FRANCES Nigh, Boniface.

FRANCES *wakes* STEPHEN.

C'mon, peh, up to bed.

STEPHEN Whah am I doin noh on your knee.

FRANCES Your Daddy was nursin ya.

STEPHEN Ya didn't tell him, did ya? Make a holy show a me.

FRANCES No, I didn't tell him.

STEPHEN I'm givin y'up for Lint, ya may puh up wud me till then.

FRANCES Alrigh, ya mane thah now, do ya?

STEPHEN I do. Will ya come up and say goodnigh to me, I'll be fierce fast.

FRANCES Alrigh, me little man.

She kisses him. He walks sleepily from the room as ARIEL *stands in the doorway.*

ARIEL Ah, Ma, leh us ouh for five minutes, will ya, want to show Stephanie the car.

FRANCES Buh ud's dark, love.

ARIEL I'll be wary. Ah, Ma, ud's me birthday, I'll be righ back.

FRANCES Ya enjiy your birthday?

ARIEL Aye, never thought I'd see sixteen.

FRANCES Swear ya were ninety.

ARIEL I know ud's mad, buh I never thought I'd make me sixteenth birthday. I've this thing abouh a girl in a graveyard, don't know where ud cem from, buh just before I go to slape and me mind's blanked ouh, this sintince kapes comin. Girl in a graveyard, girl in a graveyard, I tap ud ouh on the pilla, puts me to slape like a lullaby. Mad, isn't ud?

FRANCES Ud's somethin. G'wan then to Stephanie. I'm timin ya.

ARIEL You're a great little Ma.

> *She blows her a kiss and she's gone.* FRANCES *sits there eating the cake. Hold a minute. Then enter* FERMOY *with a CD. He puts it on. Stands there listening to it, looking at her. Dancing.*

FERMOY Ya wanted some romance, missus.

FRANCES Take more than Spanish eyes to romance me.

FERMOY (*Dances towards her, for her*) You're the wan, you're the wan. I'm just busy, busy, you're lookin ah the next Taoiseach. Go aisy on me a while, will ya, and then I'm yours agin.

FRANCES Where's me locket?

> FERMOY *takes locket from his pocket, gives it to her, dancing all the time. She examines it.*

What's your phoho doin here?

FERMOY I left in the child's phoho. Don't be getting thick over natin agin. I don't mind ya wearin a phoho of the child but noh heeself. I'm the wan should be straddlin your heart.

FRANCES And what ya do wud Charlie's phoho?

FERMOY On me desk.

FRANCES   Ud's important to remember whah has been lost.

FERMOY   (*Pulling her to him*) I know. I know.

FRANCES   Like hell, ya know. Ya don't remember yesterda, you're thah suurt of a man.

FERMOY   (*Dancing with her*) Oh, I remember everythin, don't you ever fear, buh ud's important to forget too.

> *Kisses her, a long lovely kiss. Enter* HANNAFIN, *stands there watching and listening.*

FRANCES   We started on the wrong fooh, Fermoy, no way to puh ud righ.

FERMOY   Ud was meant to be.

FRANCES   I wish I could be as certain as you. Facts are me goin wud you cost me me husband's life, me son's life and forever more me peace a mind.

FERMOY   Whah happened James and Charlie was strokes a destiny.

FRANCES   Strokes a destiny?

FERMOY   Aye, natin to do wud you or me. The man above cleared the way, is all. Ony for destiny you'd a ran back and forth between me and Charlie. Ya'd be runnin still. Ya should be grateful the chice was med for ya.

FRANCES   And James?

FERMOY   James was left field, I'll admih thah. James' death shook me to the core. And then I began to understand the God we're dalin wud. He was boulsterin us for things to come.

FRANCES   Whah things to come?

FERMOY   We mustn't be afraid, we mustn't baulk, ony dance to the music till the music's done. And when I'm Taoiseach you'll be there wud me, where ya belong. That's whah's wrong a the country, noh enough sex. I'm goin to creahe a new ministry, the ministry a sex. You'll be the minister and I'll be your assistant. We'll give em demonstrations on the national airwaves, we'll be the new Angelus.

HANNAFIN   And put the whole nation off their tay.

31

FERMOY   Hannafin . . . Whah do we owe this pleasure to?
HANNAFIN Look, Fitzgerald, ya wont geh me seah offa me. I've
          the core vohe wrapped up, whole county in me fist.
FERMOY   Four votes, Hannafin. All I naded last time, four
          votes. Thah's never happenin agin.
HANNAFIN Ya want to play dirty. Alrigh. I'm the Baron a Dirt
          when ud's called for.
FERMOY   I'm squaky clane, and ya know ud. Thah's why
          you're here whimperin like a girl.
HANNAFIN Squaky clane. Whah abouh your father and mother?
FERMOY   Whah's thah got to do wud me?
HANNAFIN Everywan knows you were there.
FERMOY   I was there alrigh. But you're noh criminally respon-
          sible ah seven. Ya don't know your law.
HANNAFIN I know me law and I know the pulse a the paple.
          The apple doesn't fall far from the tree. And here,
          I've the figures a the new poll. (*Produces fax*)
FERMOY   That's noh ouh till the mornin.
HANNAFIN For the likes a you, mebbe. For us in the know any
          information can be goh. I'm miles ahead a ya. Here,
          look ah ud yourself.
FERMOY   (*Hits it away*) Them polls, allas wrong.

HANNAFIN *smiles, lets poll sheet fall to the floor.*

HANNAFIN And how is the lady a the house?
FRANCES   Very well, thank you.
HANNAFIN Was visihin the Mother's grave today, do thah every
          Sunda, brin the auld daffodils to lay on her bones,
          and I passed be your son's grave, tiny little yoke of a
          yoke, fierce neglected lookin, reminded me a you.
          Just who do yees think yees are? Yees think the wind
          is in yeer favour just because yees built the big
          house wud the Grake columns and the fountains
          goin full blast and the lions roarin on the gates and
          the money pourin in from the cement and gravel.
          Ud's my wind yees goh a whiff of and be careful ud
          doesn't blow yees away. You're messin wud my
          votes, Fitzgerald, the hurlers on the ditch who'd go

32

wud me if you weren't banjaxin everythin. Back down now before ya make a hames of ud all. Sure they're ony laughin at ya. The murderers' son for this county. That'll never happen. Back down now and I'll owe ya wan.

FERMOY The county's sick a ya, Hannafin, and ya know ud. Ya do natin ony drink whiskey and lap-dance. Whin's the last time you spoke in the Dáil apart from tellin them to close the winda?

HANNAFIN Alrigh, I asked ya nicely. Now we'll do ud the hard way. If you don't back down I've an interview done that'll put ya in your place. All I have to do is make a call and ud'll be all over the mornin papers.

FERMOY I know what's in ud. You're noh the ony wan can geh information. Natin ony hoh air abouh me laineage. Me mother and father, Frances' son and first husband, me brother Boniface and hees addictions, long cured, ya didn't put thah in. Thah's all ya have, thah's all there is. Pathehic. Oh, aye, there's me greah grandfather, they say he ate a child durin the famine. So did everywan's durin the famine. So did yours.

HANNAFIN Well, if he did, he didn't ate wan of hees own.

FERMOY Hunger is hunger. Laineage manes natin anymore. You're the auld generation thah'd like to kape us in our place forever. We new wans comin up judge a man for whah he is in heeself, noh where he cem from. We judge a man these days be hees own merit, as if he'd ne'er a smithy bar God heeself.

HANNAFIN The pipe drames of the self-med. You were forged in a bloodbah, Fitzgerald, and the son allas carries the father somewhere inside of him. I know thah much, he carries the Da inside of him sure as he carries hees kidneys, the family jewels, the heart. And ud's time the paple beyond this parish knew the gruesome blacksmith hommered you to earth and the symmetry can be predicted from there.

FERMOY And whah abouh your own symmetry, Hannafin, and your father dancin up the field the last three year of hees life, waltzin wud the sheep, or your mother stealin jars a coffee from every shop for miles around? Whah was ud abouh coffee thah everthin collided in her over jars a coffee? Or your grandmother walkin inta the silver river ah eighy-seven? Christ, if ya could puh up wud ud all till you're eighy-seven and thah new asbestos plant, there's noh a lake or river we can swim in anymore, thanks to you. And thah piggery, who's been fundin thah all these years? There's lots a questions to be asked concernin you if ya want to play ud thah way.

HANNAFIN And there's a few inquiries to be med as to how the cement and gravel empire goh off of the ground.

FERMOY The cement and gravel was grown from the air be me and Frances and ya know ud. I heard ya been snoopin round our accounts, whadlin the tax biys, and ya found natin because there's natin to find. I'm warnin you, Hannafin, you open your gob abouh my personal life and I'll take ya to the claners.

HANNAFIN There's somethin rotten in you, Fitzgerald. I know ud, know ud like me own hand. I just can't puh a finger on ud yeh. Buh I will before long. In the manetime thah interview goes ouh in the mornin. That'll get the ball rollin. If ya've any thoughts to the contrary ya know me number. I'll give ya an hour, no more.

Exit HANNAFIN.

FRANCES (*Poll sheet*) Is these polls accurahe?

FERMOY Accurahe enough.

FRANCES Well, I'm noh looking forward to radin abouh meself in the papers. Me aunts'll go through the roof. Peg in the towel, Fermoy, ud's obvious he's goin to win. Ring him, geh him to cancel thah interview.

FERMOY A'you goin to start layin inta me as well?

FRANCES Everywan says he's goin to hould hees seah. Look, we been through this before wud Hannafin.

34

FERMOY   Ya don't same to know how important this is, missus.
FRANCES I know whah ud's like livin wud you after a defeat.
FERMOY   I'm noh losing this time. Geh thah inta your head.
FRANCES You're the ony wan thinks thah.
FERMOY   I suppose ya'd like me to lose agin.
FRANCES I'd like a bih a peace round here. I'd like a bih a
         help wud the cement. Ya know, mebbe too many
         bad things has happened, Fermoy, for you to win.
         Mebbe you losin agin is God tellin us our golden
         reprieve is over.
FERMOY   Kape your auld guilt trip to yourself. Charlie and
         James have natin to do wud this and they've natin
         to do wud me.
FRANCES You tould Charlie abouh us. You tould Charlie abouh
         us though I begged ya not to.
FERMOY   Somewan had to tell him. You weren't goin to.
FRANCES I would have. In me own time.
FERMOY   Like hell ya would. Ya'd still be stringin the both of
         us along.
FRANCES You just couldn't waih to hurt somewan. You knew
         thah man loved me.
FERMOY   And I don't?
FRANCES He was my husband. You were just a fling, a fling
         thah wint wrong.
FERMOY   Then whah're ya doin wud me this seventeen year?
FRANCES You're the father a me children. That's whah I'm
         doin wud ya.

         Exit FRANCES. FERMOY *sits there brooding. Hold a
         minute. Enter* ARIEL.

ARIEL   Meh Hannafin in the lane.
FERMOY   Aye, he was here.
ARIEL   The car's mad.
FERMOY   Is ud?
ARIEL   Yeah. Thanks. (*Kisses the top of his head*)
FERMOY   Whah'd Hannafin to say for heeself?
ARIEL   He puts wan a hees cowbiy boots up on the bonneh,
         lanes in the winda, pats me on the head, 'Aren't

35

you the fine girl, Ariel Fitzgerald, considerin who
spawned ya?' Tould me to give ya this.

FERMOY *examines it.*

Whah is ud?
FERMOY Ah, ud's an auld newspaper cuttin abouh me father's
trial.
ARIEL Whah was he really like?
FERMOY Whah was he really like? He was really like whah he
really was, a man in a navy raincoah thah butchered
me mother . . . Ya know whah he done after?
ARIEL Whah?
FERMOY Lih a cigarette, puh me up on hees shoulders, all the
way up from the lake, across the fields to the Sea
Dew Inn. We sah at the counter, him drinkin four
Jemmies, the eyes glihherin, glancin from me to the
glass to the fluur, then lanin over and whisperin
'Time to be turnin ourselves in'.
ARIEL And what did you say?
FERMOY Don't remember if I said anhin . . . All I remember is
lookin ah him, the low sounds of Sunda evenin
drinkin, the barmaid puttin an lipstick and him
smilin, yeah, smilin. How can ya describe thah to
anywan?
ARIEL He shouldn't a said 'we'.
FERMOY Ya think noh?
ARIEL A cuurse noh.
FERMOY No, 'we' was righ. I was there too. And though I was
ony seven, an excuse on this earth, I was also seven
thousand and seven millin, for the soul is wan age
and mine just stood and watched. I'd seen him
drown a bag a kittens, blind, tiny pink tongues and
fairy teeth. Really this was no different.

A pause. FERMOY *studies* ARIEL.

ARIEL Whah? Whah is ud, Daddy?
FERMOY Ya want to take me for a spin in your new chariot?

ARIEL   Alrigh. Where do ya want to go?
FERMOY   Anywhere.
ARIEL   Then anywhere ud is. Will we brin Ma?
FERMOY   Gone to bed.
ARIEL   I'll puh ouh the ligh so.

She looks out. Puts out the light. 'Mors et Vita' music. Blackout.

ACT TWO

'Mors et Vita' music as curtain comes up. Ten years later. FERMOY *sits centre stage. Beautifully groomed. An interview is in progress.* VERONA, *the interviewer, sits to the side. Cameraman, soundman, to the other side.* ELAINE *stands watching, in a suit, taking notes.*

FERMOY Yes, I've held three ministries over the past ten years.

VERONA And of the three, Minister, do you have a favourite?

FERMOY They're all very different. I enjiyed tremendously Arts and Culture though I was only there for a year. Ih was an area I knew very little abouh when I took over the brief. I used look up to artists and poets before I got to know em. Ih was a greah education to realize they're as fickle and wrongheaded as the rest of us. Thah said, ih was a huge learnin curve for me and, I'll tell ya, it's hard to beah a pride a poets and a tank a wine for good conversation.

VERONA And what is it, Minister, that's just so great about their conversation?

FERMOY It's noh aisy puh a finger on ud, buh I think ud's their attempts, mostly banjaxed mind you, buh an attempt anyway to throw eternihy on the table.

VERONA You're a great believer in eternity, aren't you, Minister?

FERMOY Yes, I am.

VERONA You said it was divine providence that won you your seat ten years ago.

FERMOY I said ih was divine grace.

VERONA With all due respects to divine grace, Minister, didn't you rise in proportion to Hannafin's fall?

FERMOY A cuurse I did, but thah doesn't diminish divine grace. If that scandal had broken a week laher, Hannafin would've kept hees seat.

VERONA There were suggestions at the time, Minister, that you were instrumental in the breaking of that scandal.

FERMOY Malicious gossip.

VERONA   And still the rumours persist, Minister.

FERMOY   Yeah, by them thah'd like to take me down. Facts are I was elected fair and square by the people. Why make a mountain ouh of a molehill?

VERONA   I wouldn't call the suicide of a highly respected politician a 'molehill', Minister.

FERMOY   I wasn't referrin to Hannafin's suicide as a 'molehill'. I was referrin to how I was elected. Hannafin's suicide was tragic. We weren't exactly bosom buddies but ud wint hard wud me thah he thought ud necessary to take hees own life. And ud has been devastatin for hees wife and children.

VERONA   No doubt it has. However, you went on to become Minister of Finance after Arts and Culture. How did you find that transition?

FERMOY   Well, there's more fiction written in Finance than in Arts and Culture, so the transition wasn't that difficult.

VERONA   I remember, Minister, the outrage at the time, both within your own Party and from the Opposition, when you were appointed. They said you were untried, untested, too green.

FERMOY   They said a loh of other things too, not fit for public consumption.

VERONA   The former Taoiseach took a big risk on you.

FERMOY   Ih turned ouh to be no risk. My term in Finance was wan of the most successful in the history of the State.

VERONA   And it begs the question why you haven't remained in Finance.

FERMOY   I'd learned all I had to learn there.

VERONA   It's on the record, Minister, that you said of Finance, and I quote, 'I'm fed up being the nation's handbag.'

FERMOY   Thah was said in a private conversation, on Christmas Eve, after seven brandies. Are ya goin to crucify me for thah now?

VERONA   You're also on the record as saying that your term in Finance left you feeling like Granny on pension day with the bag of gobstoppers.

FERMOY Look, I spent five-and-a-half year in Finance. I brough ud kickin and screamin inta the twenty-first century. I brough money inta the country from places yees didn't know existed and in ways ye'd never dreamt of. I done me service in Finance. Ih was time to move on.

VERONA But your refusal to remain in Finance caused a huge rift between you and the former Taoiseach.

FERMOY Yes, ud did, but don't forgeh I served him faithfully for the best part of eight year. He taught me everythin I know.

VERONA Was it a question, Minister, of the pupil outstripping the master?

FERMOY Ih was more complicahed than thah.

VERONA Whatever it was, it led to the no-confidence motion in his leadership last year.

FERMOY Mebbe ud did.

VERONA Come on, Minister, the whole country knows you were behind that no-confidence motion. The word abroad is that the present Taoiseach, Mr Dudley, is your puppet and that very shortly he'll get the axe too.

FERMOY Well, the word is wrong. As usual. I wish I knew as much abouh meself as yees reporters know. The facts are very different.

VERONA And what are the facts, Minister?

FERMOY There's an optimum moment for everywan, few recognize ud when ud comes and fewer still recognize when the moment is gone. Never to return. The Taoiseach was jaded. The party had lost direction and the party cannoh be sacrificed to wan individual, whahever our privahe estimations of thah individual may be. And belave me when I say I held him in the highest esteem and will always. Hard decisions cost us all and I know more than most the price a those decisions. You think I enjiyed the public humiliation of a close friend. You're wrong. You're very wrong.

VERONA   It's not over yet, is it, Minister?

FERMOY   What d'ya mean?

VERONA   Dudley's leadership has been disastrous.

FERMOY   That's a mahher of opinion.

VERONA   The electorate is losing patience, Minister. They'd rather you came clean.

FERMOY   I've no idea what you're talkin abouh.

VERONA   That you have your eye on the leadership. That it's only a matter of time before Dudley goes. The Party's in such a state right now they'll give you the reins. That you've the whole place in uproar. You control the Cabinet as it is. You are Taoiseach in everything but name.

FERMOY   You overestimahe my power. I'm Minister for Education. That's my job.

VERONA   Can you categorically state you will not be orchestrating a no-confidence motion in Mr Dudley's leadership in the next week or two?

FERMOY   That's somethin for the Party to decide.

VERONA   Could you answer the question, please, Minister? Are you or are you not interested in Leadership?

FERMOY   Well, a cuurse I'm interested. I wouldn't be where I am if I wasn't. But I'm noh interested in power ah any price. I love power, yes, I love ud, buh I love ud as an artist loves ud.

VERONA   You love power as an artist loves it. You're quoting Napoleon, Minister.

FERMOY   I'm paraphrasin him.

VERONA   Are you comparing yourself with Napoleon, Minister?

FERMOY   Who can compare wud Napoleon? I can't, aven if I wanted to, because I'm born inta the wrong century, surrounded be the wrong people. If you're a Napoleon lover you'll know whah he said as he was dyin on St Helena, 'If I had sailed for Ireland instead of Egypt, where would England be now, and the world?' This country has missed ouh on everythin, overlooked be Alexander the Greah, overlooked be Caesar, overlooked be the Moors. Overlooked,

overlooked, overlooked. The rest a the world gets
Napoleon, we get a boatload a Vikings, a handful a
Normans and the English. We get the nation a
shopkeepers.

VERONA Napoleon's verdict on the British. Are you anti-
British, Minister?

FERMOY No, a cuurse I'm noh. I'm talkin abouh imagination.
If ya have to be colonized ya migh as well be
colonized by somewan wud a bih a vision. I'm
talkin abouh a way of lookin at the world. D'ya
look ah ud from behind a till or d'ya look ah ud
from the saddle of a horse on a battlefield? And,
like ud or noh, the legacy the Brihish have left us is
the till, whereas for Napoleon the world was wan
big battlefield. He talked abouh hees battlefields
like they were women. Which a the battlefields
was more beauhiful than the other. That's the stuff
we nade to learn, or rather re-learn, we knew ud
wance. Aven Caesar while butcherin the Celts had
to acknowledge whah a strange tribe he was dalin
wud. 'They measure periods a time be nights, noh
be days.' That's whah he said abouh us. Wance we
had a calendar, markin out time be the nigh. Them
were the biys had the perspective. Look, the
outsize ego a this nation is built on sand and wind,
a few dramers, natin else. We nade to go back to
first principles. We nade to re-imagine ourselves
from scratch.

VERONA You've been much criticized by the Opposition
for precisely this going back to first principles,
Minister, which you've outlined in your Education
Papers.

FERMOY It's the Oppositions's job to oppose so I don't take
them too seriously.

VERONA They're not the only ones unhappy over some of
the contents of these Papers.

FERMOY I'm noh interested in cosmehics. If you're goin to
do somethin, do ud righ or don't do ud ah all.
Learned thah on me mother's knee. Look, I chose

to go inta Education. Lots has seen thah as a step down. Well, ud's noh. I chose Education because ud all begins and ends wud education. And my business righ now is to re-educahe a nation. Thah won't be done in a day.

VERONA Some of us think we don't need to be re-educated, Minister, not to mind your refusal to consult with the experts. A sizeable portion of the public is alarmed by the last three Papers your party has pushed through.

FERMOY There's natin to be alarmed abouh. I think we've proved over and over we have this country's interests at heart.

VERONA But your Theology Paper, Minister, has caused uproar.

FERMOY I belave in God well as the next.

VERONA Come on, Minister, your God is as far from the traditional notion of God as it is possible to be.

FERMOY Yes, he is, and I make no apology for thah.

VERONA The Church has spoken out against you on several occasions, and I quote a recent statement from the Archbishop's office. 'What the Minister proposes is the antithesis of the nature of God. What he proposes is ancient, barbaric, and will take us back to the caves.'

FERMOY What does he mane take us back to the caves? Does he think we've left em?

FRANCES *enters, coat, briefcase, stands listening.*

VERONA The statement refers to your Paper on the nature of Christ. Could you clarify what you meant by that Paper, Minister?

FERMOY I though ih was clear enough ah the time. I was talkin abouh the sullen nature a Christ, somethin thah has been hushed up for centuries. Somethin I'd long suspected and was brough home to me by a particular paintin by Piero della Francesca. His 'Resurrection'. Puts manners on them thah tries to tell us that the deah a Christ was for us. That the resurrection a Christ was for us. Let's noh mix words here. The deah a Christ was by us, noh for us, and the resurrection a Christ was for heeself. Look ah this paintin and you'll see whah I mane. It's magnificent. A big, cranky, vengeful son a God plants a leg like a tree on hees new opened tomb. He looks ouh inta the middle distance and hees eyes say wan thing and wan thing only. Ye'll pay for this. Ye'll pay for this. No forgiveness in them eyes. The opposihe. Rage, and a staggerin sense a betrayal, as if he's sayin, I've wasted Eternihy on ye band a troglodytes thah calls yeerselves the human race. Children should be taught this along wud Barney. So I get shot down for tryin to introduce a little balance inta the education system. Well, I'm used to bein crihicized and thankfully I don't suffer from the national disase.

VERONA And what's that, Minister?

FERMOY Wantin to be liked. Ya'd swear thah was the politician's job these days. To be liked. Well, ud's noh. The politician's job is to have a vision and to push thah vision through, for wudouh a vision the people perish.

VERONA I suppose, Minister, whatever else they say about you, you're not afraid to speak your mind.

FERMOY Ud's ony slaves thah fear to speak their mind.

VERONA Perhaps. Ten years ago, Minister, you were running a cement factory and now you're tipped as the next Taoiseach. Do you ever stop for a minute and say to yourself, this is a dream?

FERMOY Well, ud's all a drame, isn't ud? Wan beauhiful heart-breakin drame, but, no, I don't ever stop, and I'll tell ya why. Fate gev me the hand, I hardly have to play ud.

VERONA And the hand fate dealt you hasn't always been so good, has it, Minister?

FERMOY No, ud hasn't.

VERONA Alongside what can only be described as your

meteoric rise is a huge personal tragedy.

FERMOY Yes . . . Ariel.

VERONA Your daughter. I know this is difficult, but could you tell us what happened to Ariel?

FERMOY Ariel walked ouha this house on her sixteenth birthday to show a friend her new car that we'd goh her as a present. She never cem home.

VERONA They never found her?

FERMOY They never found her, no.

VERONA Have you given up hope, Minister?

FERMOY Yes, I have.

VERONA You believe she's dead.

FERMOY I know she is.

VERONA How do you know, Minister?

FERMOY In me bones. Don't ask me how I know, buh I know and wish I didn't and wish ud was otherwise. I would give me life for her to walk through thah duur agin. Buh that's noh goin to happen.

VERONA It's an appalling thing at the centre of your lives.

FERMOY You have no idea.

VERONA Thank you, Minister.

FERMOY Thank you.

VERONA (Stretches. To Cameraman) You got all that? (Cameraman nods)

FERMOY Elaine, what do ya think?

ELAINE Three things. Ya can't admih ya love power. Thah has to go. God. Paple's fierce touchy abouh God. We may pare thah back. And three, Ariel. Ariel's your trump card. Play ud. Ya nade to go wud the emotion of ud more. Thah's whah paple wants, details of your personal life. Don't be afraid to give ud to em. Don't be afraid to give em Ariel.

VERONA No, no, the Ariel section was fine. If you want people to feel for you, you hold back a bit yourself. Your instincts are spot-on there, Minister.

ELAINE I'm noh so sure, buh I'm prepared to lave Ariel the way ud is if ya edit the lovin power bih and the God speech.

VERONA All right. I'll pull back a bit on God without losing the whole thing, but the loving power stays. I think it's refreshing to hear a politician admit they love power. Everyone knows you do. What's the big deal?

ELAINE Dudley'll be gone by Friday. We have to geh this wan righ. Daddy?

FERMOY Lave ud. Migh as well be hung for a sheep as a lamb.

VERONA Great.

ELAINE There's a bite to ate in the conservatory. (*Hands papers to* FERMOY) Sign these.

FERMOY Whah have we here?

ELAINE Ya can just sign. I've been over em.

FERMOY I'll jine ya in a minuhe, Verona.

> *Exit* VERONA *and* ELAINE. FERMOY *gets up, throws the papers aside, stretches, turns, sees* FRANCES.

Ah, Frances.

FRANCES How do you know she's dead?

FERMOY Ten years, Frances, ten years.

FRANCES Buh ud was the way ya said ud. Ya sounded so certain.

FERMOY Nowan shows up after ten years.

FRANCES And now she's your trump card. I thought her memory would be more . . . sacred to ya. Today is her tenth anniversary. Have you no respect?

FERMOY I know today is her tenth anniversary. Why d'ya think I'm here?

FRANCES You're here because the press has descended like crows on the church to phohograph the big bronze lug a ya glowerin inta your daugher's empty grave. Ariel's a good phoho opportunihy. The gravin father wud hees arms tightly around the gravin mother. Don't you touch me ah her Mass this avenin. I'm goin up to geh changed. Ud's ah six.

FERMOY I know ud's ah six.

FRANCES Ya'd never think ud.

> *Exit* FRANCES. FERMOY *looks after her, begins signing papers, lights a cigar, puts on a CD, dances around,*

smoking, drinking, signing papers. STEPHEN *appears in the doorway, dressed in black.*

FERMOY Stephen, ya look like an undertaker.

STEPHEN Ud's the way Ma wants ud.

FERMOY Anhin strange?

STEPHEN Naw . . . Yourself?

FERMOY I'd love to walk down Grafton Streeh and just drink coffee. Sick a watchin other people live. I'd love to walk inta a shop and buy me own newspaper and then noh read ud, forgeh ud somewhere. Were ya at the match on Sunda?

STEPHEN Ya know I've no interest in Ga.

FERMOY Well, you're the first Fitzgerald thah hasn't. How's college?

STEPHEN *shrugs.*

You're graduatin this year, aren't ya?

STEPHEN Yeah.

FERMOY Ya studyin?

STEPHEN Yeah.

FERMOY Ya never call inta see me anymore.

STEPHEN You're busy.

FERMOY Not thah busy. Drop inta me next week, we'll go for lunch.

STEPHEN There's no pint.

FERMOY Why noh?

STEPHEN Because ya'll cancel ud.

FERMOY Ah, Stephen, Stephen, Stephen, you're all grown, when did thah happen?

BONIFACE (*We hear him before we see him*) Lilies for the dead. Lilies. Lilies for sale. Lilies for the dead. Whihe lilies for all the whihe dead.

Enter BONIFACE.

STEPHEN How is Boniface?

BONIFACE Don't ever geh auld, Stephen, promise me thah.

47

STEPHEN   Thah's a promise.

And exit STEPHEN.

FERMOY   I thought you were above in Pat's dryin ouh.
BONIFACE   And I could die up there before you'd come visih
me. Pour us wan a your fortified, rectified, sancti-
fied thousand-year-auld brandies there like a good
lad.
FERMOY   I haven't been called a good lad since the last time I
seen you.
BONIFACE   Well, mebbe ya should see me more. If natin else I'd
remind ya of where ya cem ouh of.

Enter FRANCES, *dressed in black, coat, handbag.*

FRANCES   Boniface. Was wonderin would ya show.
BONIFACE   Haven't missed Ariel's anniversary yeh. Used to be
the birth a Christ was the big wan. Gets whittled
down, ud all gets whittled down. Now ud's the
death a me niece is the feast a feasts.
FERMOY   Ring a taxi and have him driven back to Pat's.
FRANCES   Ring wan yourself.

BONIFACE *has moved to drinks cabinet, about to pour.*

FERMOY   (*Stays his hand*) You've had enough, sir.
FRANCES   Give him a drink. Give him a drink. Let somewan be
intoxicahed round here. (*Pours for* BONIFACE) I drink
to forgeh buh wud each glass ud all comes clearer.
BONIFACE   Does ud?
FRANCES   Too clear, too clear to bear.
BONIFACE   For Ariel (*lilies*). Grew em meself. Stripped the hoh
house this mornin. I know her grave is empty. We
do these things for ourselves.
FRANCES   They're lovely, Boniface, thanks. (*Lays them on the
table, straightens them*)
BONIFACE   May God have mercy on your carcass, and may he
have mercy on mine. Up Offaly. (*Drinks. Pours*

*another, stands at drinks cabinet, drinking and pouring,
pouring and drinking*)

FERMOY (*Watching* FRANCES *fixing the flowers*) Ya miss me ah
all?

FRANCES Miss ya?

FERMOY Tell the truth for wance in your life.

FRANCES Alrigh. Yeah, I miss ya, noh you in yourself, noh
you now and the riddled pelt a ya, buh the
spangled idea I had a ya which is the best part a
love.

FERMOY I miss you too.

FRANCES Aye, wud your cartload a virgins spread across five
continents.

FERMOY You're noh exactly livin like a nun yourself.

FRANCES I bed the min whin the fancy takes me which isn't
often.

FERMOY Ya tryin to make me jealous?

FRANCES I'm past your jealousy. Way past.

FERMOY They're welcome to ya, snow quane that y'are, turn
any man to ice. You're noh the ony wan is beddin
them down. I've more women than votes linin up
for me. Beauhiful young women, bodies a bronze,
minds a gold, sophisticahed, beauhiful women,
teeth like delph, high-bellied, tauh as fish on a line.
And ya know somethin? They like me. Ud's ony
here I'm treahed like a dog. I step out this duur and
I'm a king.

FRANCES (*Pushes him violently*) Then go to your high-bellied
hoors. You're safer wud them and whah they don't
know about ya.

Exit FRANCES. FERMOY *stands there looking after
her.* BONIFACE *watches him from the drinks cabinet.*

BONIFACE Tell me this and tell me no more, was ud worth ud?

FERMOY Was whah worth ud?

BONIFACE And whah about me?

FERMOY Whah about ya?

BONIFACE You tould me, ony I didn't understand what ya

were sayin, ya tould me, Fermoy, thah nigh ya were goin an abouh blood sacrifice, in this very room.

FERMOY I've no idea what you're talkin abouh.

BONIFACE No. No. Listen. Listen. Listen. I can't stop drinkin. Can't slape, can't ate, garden be moonligh, go to bed in the mornin. I'm afraid I'll tell me psychiatrist, thah it'll just spill ouha me. They don't know what's wrong a me. Me soul, I tell em, me soul ud's hurtin me fierce, like bein flayed from the inside. They think I'm some suurt a religious nuh. Burst a blood vessel in me eye, bled blood down me face for two days, they couldn't stop ud. You're the wan should be in Pat's. You're the wan should be bleedin from the eyes.

FERMOY Take ud aisy, take ud aisy, you're ouh a your mind wud drink and tranquilizers. Take ud aisy.

BONIFACE Take ud aisy! I'm facin me maker wud this on me immortal soul. Do you aven realize whah ya've done! Why didn't ya listen to me when I tried to stop ya, though I didn't know whah I was tryin to stop. Why didn't ya listen? All we have in this world is the small mercies we can extend to wan another. The rest is madness and oblivion. Haven't ya learnt thah much? Haven't ya learnt thah much on your travels?

FERMOY Oh, aye, I learnt thah much alrigh, but like everythin worth learnin, ud's learnt too lahe. Everythin comes when you've no more use for ud, must be a law.

FRANCES *at the door in her coat.*

FRANCES We're goin to be lahe, geh an your mournin, will ya.

FERMOY Don't you talk to me abouh mournin. (*Takes out electric shaver, mirror, shaves himself*) Most gets up offa the ground sooner or laher, dusts themselves down, rejines the land a the livin. Not you though. Everythin thah happens to Frances Fitzgerald has to be momentous, spectacular. Her jiys could never be the same as anywan else's and her grafes must be inconsolable. Live! Live! Live! That's whah we're here for. Do somethin! Anhin! Ya'll have all of eternihy for pussin in the dark.

FRANCES You're noh browbatin the Opposition now.

FERMOY Amn't I? . . . This funeral parlour I come home to every time.

FRANCES Ya were home wance this year. Two hours for your Christmas dinner.

Enter ELAINE, *dressed in black, holds out mobile.*

ELAINE Himself wants a quick word.

FERMOY (*Takes phone*) Will ya organize thah fella back to where he cem from. (*On the phone*) Boss . . . No harm done . . . Whah is ud?

And exit FERMOY.

ELAINE What ya want to do, Boniface?

BONIFACE I'll go back to Pat's after Mass.

ELAINE Alrigh, I'll drive ya, goin back tonigh meself.

FRANCES (*Sitting, muttering, drink, coat on, handbag*) Twinty-six . . . twinty-six years of age . . . (*Shakes her head*)

BONIFACE Whah?

FRANCES Ariel . . . She'd be twinty-six if she was here today . . . I don't think I slept a nigh straight when I was carryin her. Had meself convinced I didn't deserve her on account a James. Kept thinkin this child's goin to come ouh wrong, this child's goin to come ouh wrong. Nighmare ridin nighmare she be deformed, no face on her or wan a thim frog babbies or birdy-headed little creatures ya see phohos of, or she was goin to have no arms or die ah the last minuhe as happens oftener than paple knows. Buh ouh she cem wud everythin ya nade to look human. And for ages after I'd look ah her and whisper, thank you, God, thank you, God. For along wud the night sweats I still dared to hope I be given another chance. And for a while I thought I had. Buh the man above was ony playin wud me . . . ony playin wud me, is all.

ELAINE And did ya have nighmares when ya carried me?

FRANCES No, belave ud or noh, you were aisy. The trouble wud you started after ya were born. Though I had to have a jar a beetroot every nigh when I was carryin you. I'd wake up in the middle a the nigh dyin for beetroot . . . Kept a jar beside the bed. 'Another beetroot party, missus?' Fermoy'd guffaw from under the quilt. Buh I didn't care, I'd sih there in the dark atin beetroot and then I'd drink the vinegar. Mebbe that's why you're so bihher.

ELAINE Am I bihher, Ma?

FRANCES As a field a lemons.

ELAINE Sure ud's noh yourself you're talkin abouh and ya shrunk to a pip over your two dead children.

FRANCES You'd have me forgeh em like your father.

ELAINE I'd have ya cut your grafe accordin to your cloth.

FRANCES You'd have me grave to a timetable, throw Ariel and James aside like a pair of auld gloves or an umbrella left after the rain.

ELAINE Your empire a sorrow doesn't convince me and ya cuttin dales like a shark down ah the cement every day a the wake. Ya switch ud on, Ma, ya switch ud on when ud suits.

FRANCES And whah would you know abouh sorrow and ya dry-eyed at your sister's funeral?

ELAINE I know wan thing abouh sorrow. I learned ud watchin you. Sorrow's an addiction like no other. You won't be full till you've buried us all. Well, ya won't bury me, Ma. I'm here, thrivin, your unlovely daugher is thrivin, your unlovely daugher that ya'd swap like thah for Ariel to return. She's noh comin home, Ma. She's noh comin home. Ud's just me now, me and Stephen.

FRANCES How do you know she's noh comin home?

ELAINE Thah's none a your business.

FRANCES Do you have information you're kapin from me?

ELAINE And if I had?

FRANCES You and your father, swear ya were married to him. You tell me now what you know!

ELAINE I know natin, Ma, natin ya don't know yourself.

Enter SARAH.

SARAH Ah, Boniface, ya do a runner agin?

BONIFACE The savage loves hees nahive shore.

SARAH And what d'ya think a the antics a your little brother? They're goin to puh him on the throne. I used change that fella's nappy. Seen ud all now. (*Watches as* BONIFACE *pours another drink for himself*) Ya were thirsty as a child too, a bottle in each fist as ya snoozed in the coh. Your Ma used love watchin ya guzzlin. The little sounds of him, she used say, isn't he like a little bonamh?

BONIFACE You'd reminiss the future, missus, if ya though ya'd geh away wud ud.

SARAH Aye, I would and noh wan a yees would belave me.

STEPHEN *has entered.*

STEPHEN It's ten to six.

ELAINE Give him a minuhe. We'll make ud, they'll wait for us.

BONIFACE Stephen, I hear you're the new John Ford.

STEPHEN I wish.

ELAINE He won a prize and all.

BONIFACE Didn't I rade about ud in the paper.

STEPHEN That's ony because a Daddy.

BONIFACE A prize is a prize. These things is important. Never won as much as a turkey meself. Whah was the film abouh anyway?

STEPHEN Ma'll tell ya, she's fierce proud of ud.

FRANCES Ah, ud was disgustin, Stephen, no two ways abouh ud. Near fainted when I seen ud. Ya've this mother and her son and ud's the son's weddin day and then the son goes missin, and the bride is lookin all over the hotel for her new husband. And where does she find her new husband? In the bridal suihe, on the bridal bed, bein breast-fed be the mother. Now what's thah abouh, I ask ya? What's the pint in makin a film about thah?

STEPHEN Does there allas have to be a pint, Ma?

FRANCES I'll tell ya what the pint was. The pint was to geh at me.

STEPHEN You think everthin comes back to you. Ud doesn't.

FRANCES Then why did ya call the mother Frances in your film? Why was she dressed like me? Why was she drivin an auld Merc? That's whah I drive. I don't nade this, Stephen. Pack a lies, the whole thing.

STEPHEN Ud's noh a pack a lies. Ud happened.

FRANCES Didn't happen here, me bucko.

STEPHEN Buh ud happened. Read abouh ud in an Italian newspaper. Ya don't have to make anhin up.

BONIFACE Thah's for sure. Everythin ya can possibly imagine has happened already or, if ud hasn't, will shortly.

FRANCES And manetime the cement is waitin on ya.

STEPHEN I'll puh a bullet through me head first.

FERMOY *stands in the doorway. He has changed into his mourning clothes.*

FERMOY Righ, are we off?

FRANCES You come back here after Mass. Don't go scurryin away, ya hear?

FERMOY I've a seven o'clock meetin in the mornin.

FRANCES You come back here or I'll folly ya to Dublin. (*To the others, exiting*) Come an, we're lahe, we're lahe.

Exit FRANCES *followed by* BONIFACE *and* STEPHEN.

ELAINE A'ya alrigh, Daddy?

FERMOY Your mother.

ELAINE Don't mind her, brazen ud ouh, we'll be gone straih

54

after Mass, won't have to see her for another year.

FERMOY Have Bernard drive yees down. I'll walk.

ELAINE We should all arrive together.

FERMOY I nade two minutes to meself, Elaine.

ELAINE Alrigh, alrigh, I'll send Bernard back for ya.

Exit ELAINE. SARAH *pours a whiskey for herself.*

FERMOY Ya noh goin down to dunk your soul?

SARAH A millin Masses wouldn't bleach ud.

FERMOY Nor mine.

SARAH Nor yours. (*Raises* FERMOY's *chin with her hand*) That's ih. Never leh em see ya wud the harness off.

Exit SARAH. FERMOY *stands there a moment, gets out pocket mirror, checks himself in it, teeth, hair, eyes, a long look.*

FERMOY Who are ya, sir? Who are ya and from where do ya come? Geh a hould, stranger, geh a hould. (*Clicks mirror shut. Takes a deep breath*) Righ, let's rock and roll.

The phone rings. Note on ARIEL's *voice: once convention of the phone has been established, let* ARIEL's *voice come from everywhere.* FERMOY *does not talk into the phone after the first couple of exchanges.*

Yes?

ARIEL Hello.

FERMOY Elaine, I'm on the way, tell her I'm on the way.

ARIEL Ud's me.

FERMOY Who's me?

ARIEL Me, Ariel.

FERMOY Ariel . . . Who is this? I'm in no mood for . . .

ARIEL No, ud's me, Ariel.

FERMOY Buh ud can't be . . . ud can't.

ARIEL Buh ud is.

FERMOY Oh, Ariel . . . you're alive . . . you're alive.

ARIEL Come and get me, will ya? Ud's awful here, ud's awful. There's a huge pike after me, he lives in the belfry, two rows a teeth on him and teeth on hees tongue, bendin back to hees throah. He won't rest till he has me. Come and get me, will ya?

FERMOY How? Tell me how can I come and get ya?

ARIEL (*Sounds of terrible weeping*) I don't know . . . I want to go home . . . I just want to go home. Please, just brin me home.

FERMOY Ariel . . . Ariel . . . don't . . . don't.

> *He listens as sound of* ARIEL's *weeping fades and fades to silence.* FERMOY *stands there. Let him stand there, utterly still, looking out. Then enter* FRANCES. *She stands in the doorway, in her coat, out of breath.* FERMOY *registers her after a while. They look at one another for an age.*

FERMOY Ya cem back for me. I'm comin, I'm comin.

FRANCES No more Masses.

FERMOY Well, I'm goin. Where's Bernard? Come an and we get this over wud.

FRANCES You're goin nowhere. Ud was you, wasn't ud? Ud was you.

FERMOY Y'ony realizin thah now? I thought ya knew for years.

FRANCES Knew whah for years?

FERMOY Frances . . . ya didn't . . . Look this is noh the time for this conversation.

FRANCES You. Allas you and me scourin the world for her. You. And me gone to ground wud grafe. You. And ony last nigh I dreamt she walked in the duur and ten year a madness just fell away. She had wan life. Wan. Are you tellin me you took ud?

FERMOY Ariel was a drame hopped among us from start to end. We had the privelege of her company a while buh she was never really ours. We brough somethin inta the world thah didn't belong here and so we gev her back.

FRANCES Gev her back? We gev her back? Gev her back where?

FERMOY Remember them wings she was born wud?

FRANCES Wings? Whah wings?

FERMOY Them wings on her shoulder blades.

FRANCES Whah are ya talkin abouh? Whah wings? On her shoulder blades? Them growths on her shoulders, is thah what you're talkin abouh?

FERMOY They were the start a wings.

FRANCES They were balls a hardened bone and gristle, thah's all, benign, tiny, we had em removed.

FERMOY You're callin them everthin except what they were. Leh me tell you somethin, Frances. Before I ever laid eyes on you, long before thah, I had a drame, a drame so beauhiful I wanted to stay in ud till the end a time. I'm in a yella cuurtyard wud God and we're chewin the fah and then this girl wud wings appears by hees side. And I say, who owns her? And God says she's his. And I say, give us the loan of her, will ya? No, he says, she's noh earth flavour, like he's talkin abouh ice-crame. And stupidly I say, I'll take her anyway. Alrigh, he says, smilin ah me rale sly, alrigh, buh remember this is a loan. I know, I know, I says, knowin natin. And the time'll come when I'll want her returned, he says. Yeah, yeah, I say, fleein the cuurtyard wud her before he changes hees mind. Ariel. Thah was Ariel.

FRANCES Just tell me where she is.

FERMOY I'm tellin ya, thah was Ariel I fled the cuurtyard wud. And then I wake and the enchantment begins. You, Ariel, Elaine, Stephen. All the trinkets of this world showered on us. We had ten good years, hadn't we? Them were the years and we didn't know ud. He gev, he gev, he gev, and then like the tide he turned and took ud all away.

FRANCES (*A heartbroken wail, weeping like we've never seen, stands there heaving and choking and wailing*) Ariel . . . Ariel . . . Ariel . . . How could ya? . . . You loved thah child . . . How could ya? (*Shakes him*)

FERMOY I had to! I had to!

FRANCES You had to!

FERMOY Yeah, I had to. Ya think I wanted to sacrifice Ariel?
I had to.

FRANCES Sacrifice? Ya sacrificed her? What did you do to her?

FERMOY I tould ya I returned her to where she cem from.

FRANCES She cem from here, from you, from me.

FERMOY She rode ouha God from nowhere and to God she
returned.

FRANCES You sacrificed her! Aaaagh. Why didn't ya sacrifice yourself if he wanted a sacrifice? Why didn't
ya refuse?

FERMOY A cuurse I refused. I fough him till I couldn't figh
him anymore.

FRANCES Thah was no God ya med your pact wud. No God
demands such things.

FERMOY My God did.

FRANCES Blem God, blem the world, anywan bar yourself.
Ud's all comin clear now, clear as a bell. Ya done
ud for power, didn't ya, some voodoo swap in the
dark for power. You laid my daughter on an altar
for power. You've flourished these ten years since
Ariel. You've flourished on her white throat. You
swapped her to advance.

FERMOY Yes, I did. Yes, I did. I had to. Ud was the price
demanded.

FRANCES And you dare to stand here tellin me fairy stories
abouh her.

FERMOY Frances, I know whah I have done. I know my
portion a blame, buh when I'm hauled before him
I'll fling hees portion ah him, where ud belongs. I
have lived my life by hees instructions. He asked
the unaskable and I obeyed, and then he departs,
lavin me here in ashes. And my greahest fear is he
won't be there whin I go. No, I've wan greaher,
thah he will.

FRANCES (Softly) Buh Ariel . . . Fermoy . . . This is Ariel
you're talkin abouh.

FERMOY Don't make ud more difficult for me than ud is.

FRANCES Ya med ud difficult yourself. This was your playground well as anywan's.

FERMOY This is no playground and never was. This is where he hunts us down like deer and flays us alive for sport.

FRANCES Whah was ud I seen the day I first wint wud you?

FERMOY I'll tell ya what ya seen. Ya seen a man capable of anhin. And thah seh fire to your little bungalow life. Ya seen a man that could do away wud your children and ya ran towards him, noh away from him. That's whah drew ya the first time and that's what kapes ya swirlin round me. Tombstones, headstones, graveyard excitement and the promise of funerals to come.

FRANCES You'll say anhin for company in your carnage.

FERMOY You wanted me, missus, and ya still want me. Ud's ony your pride is stoppin ya.

FRANCES I wanted me first husband. Was through wud you before the honeymoon started. You stole me life from me, me children from me, everythin I though I was from me and I a glazed fool flung open the duurs for the plunder. Never agin.

FERMOY You want a divorce? Yours for the askin.

FRANCES Ya think ya'll geh off thah aisy? Where is she?

FERMOY Thah you'll never know.

FRANCES I cem from gintle people, me father used rescue spiders from the bah, mice he'd carry ouh in hees hand and leh go in the field, gintle people, Charlie, James, Ariel, gintle, gintle, gintle, no place for em in this nest a hooves. Where is she? (*Stabs him*)

FERMOY (*Reels*) Frances.

FRANCES (*Another stab*) Where is she?

FERMOY You think you can do away wud me . . . Gimme thah.

A struggle. FRANCES *stabs him again.*

FRANCES And you thought I was afraid a the knife. (*Another stab*) Where is she?

FERMOY (*Falls to the ground. She gets on top of him*) No . . .
Frances . . . no . . . Stop . . . stop . . .

FRANCES And did you stop when Ariel cried ouh for mercy?
Did ya? Tell me where she is.

FERMOY This wasn't . . . this . . . Sweet God in your . . .

FRANCES Tell me. Where is she?

FERMOY (*Whispers as he dies*) Cuura Lake.

FRANCES Cuura Lake.

> *She throws down the knife. 'Mors et Vita' music, and
> blackout.*

ACT THREE

'Mors et Vita' music continues from end of Act Two. Two months later. A coffin lies centre stage. ELAINE *lies on the floor in T-shirt and tracksuit bottoms. She's asleep. A drink beside her. Enter* STEPHEN, *suit, folders, takes in the coffin, goes to it, has a long look.*

STEPHEN   Elaine . . . Elaine . . . (*Shakes her gently*) Ya should go up to bed.

ELAINE   Ah, Stephen. (*Yawns*)

STEPHEN   When did ud arrive?

ELAINE   This mornin . . . (*Stretching*) What time is ud?

STEPHEN   After five.

ELAINE   Oh, God. (*Lies down again*)

STEPHEN   (*Goes back to coffin*) Thought she'd be behher preserved, Cuura Lake bein a bog lake and all.

ELAINE   She looked behher when they took her up first. Forensics scraped her down.

STEPHEN   Hard to square this wud Daddy.

ELAINE   Ya think?

STEPHEN   Don't you?

ELAINE   I knew for a while ud was him.

STEPHEN   Did ya?

ELAINE   Didn't you?

STEPHEN   No, a few stray thoughts. Never wahered them. How did ya know?

ELAINE   He tould me . . . Well, I asked him abouh her wan time. Venice. Some conference. Drink on the table in a little restaurant lookin on to the Rialto. And he tould me the whole thing. Very emotional he was too. Ariel was the stroke a destiny, he said, woven into him from the beginnin. Ariel was Necessity udself, the thing thah's decided ouhside a time. And he tould me all abouh Necessity. How before ya come to this world, Necessity and her sisters

61

weaves a carpet for ya. And ya watch as they weave so ya know how things will fare ouh below. And then ya turn your back and Necessity puts a twist in the weave. Thah's the wan thing ya can't foresee and thah's the wan thing will define your stay here. And then you're flung to earth wud this weave and this twist in the weave thah some calls fate.

STEPHEN Ya belave thah?

ELAINE Belaved ud thah nigh. The lights on the waher, ud's hard to be rational in Venice.

STEPHEN Ma wants to puh her in beside Daddy.

ELAINE If thah wan as much as touches a pebble of my father's grave.

STEPHEN Well, you shouldn't a puh up thah headstone, her name noh even on ud. Ma wanted to puh up hees headstone. You're like an alsatian the way ya guard hees grave.

ELAINE And you're still slurpin ah her altar after all she's done.

STEPHEN There was a pair a them in ud. She keeps askin for ya, Elaine, to go visih her. Ya wouldn't know her. She's still our mother.

ELAINE Ariel's the ony wan she cares abouh. Ariel and James, her dead children, while she bates her livin inta the dirt.

STEPHEN Thah's noh true, sick a ya givin ouh abouh her.

ELAINE And I'm sick a you makin your weekly pilgrimages to her, brinin information abouh me. I warned ya noh to tell her anhin abouh me. I'll live like a tinker in me own house if I want, me father's house. She's natin to me anymore. Natin.

STEPHEN Well, ya certainly proved thah, ravin agin her in cuurt.

ELAINE Ya know I wish I'd said more agin her.

STEPHEN A spew a lies.

ELAINE I tould ud as ud happened.

STEPHEN Like hell ya did. Anyway ud's been struck.

ELAINE I knew ud would, buh ud was still heard. You don't seem to understand whah's goin on here, Stephen.

She killed our father, slashed him till blood ran down the walls. I had to bury him in pieces. I was the only mourner ah hees funeral. Me, Boniface, Auntie Sarah. You were too busy swaddlin Ma to go to your own father's funeral. Such as ud was. She wouldn't aven allow him a public funeral. Paple loved Daddy. You saw the size a the removal. She aven tried to stop thah. But she couldn't. They just kept comin.

STEPHEN They kept comin to have a gawk.

ELAINE They cem because they loved him. You never seen Daddy in hees element. You never seen him the way he seen himself, the way he was born to be seen, the way he could work a room, the way he held himself when he spoke, the big mellifluous vice, ya'd hear a pin drop. He was goin to run this country. He was goin to cahapult the whole nation ouha sleaze and sentimentalihy and gombeenism. I'm goin to take this country to the moon, he used say to me, and he would've, ony for her. And she's still noh happy havin done away wud him. No, now she had ud in her head to take away hees name and mine wud ud and yours, though ya don't seem to care. Draggin this yoke up ouha Cuura Lake. All to destriy what's left of hees reputation. All to make her look like a martyr.

Enter FRANCES *and* BONIFACE.

STEPHEN Ma, we weren't expectin ya till tonigh.

FRANCES They let me ouh early to avide the press. Hello, Elaine.

ELAINE *looks at her.*

I was hopin we could be civil for Ariel's funeral.

ELAINE Were ya?

63

FRANCES *goes to coffin. Looks. Leans in. Kisses* ARIEL.
Leans in for ages.

FRANCES (*Whispers*) Ya'll soon be the girl in the graveyard ya
tould me abouh wance. Ya'll soon rest aisy. Who
picked ouh her dress?

STEPHEN Elaine did.

FRANCES Thank you.

ELAINE Was in her wardrobe. They had to staple ud on to
her. I didn't do ud for you.

BONIFACE Elaine. Elaine. Elaine.

ELAINE You're goin to geh off on insanihy, a cuurse y'are, ya
can shooh a baby in the face these days and geh off
on insanihy.

FRANCES Well, if I do ud'll be no thanks to you.

ELAINE Ud was murder. Cold-blooded murder, and if you
geh off on insanihy I'll open me own cuurtroom
here.

FRANCES You weren't aven here and ya med out ya were.

ELAINE I was here. He died in my arms. You were standin in
the hall lookin at the radiahor.

FRANCES And would you have done different if he done to
wan a yours whah he done to Ariel?

ELAINE Yes, I would.

FRANCES Oh, ya would, would ya?

ELAINE Yes, I would. I can tell the difference between a
crime of eternihy and a low, blood-spahhered, knife-
frenzied revenge. And then your coward's insanihy
plea on top of ud. Whah my father done to Ariel had
the grandeur a God in ud. Pure sacrifice. Ferocious,
aye. Buh pure. Whah you done to him was a
puckered, vengeful, self-servin thing wud noh a
whiff of the immortal in ud.

FRANCES So your father spills blood and he's a haroh. I spill
ud and I'm a coward. You've spint too long around
the min, me girl, too long cavortin the corriduurs a
power to understand the first thing abouh justice. Ya
know, there's ony wan thing I regreh. Thah I didn't
do ud sooner. And I won't apologize to you for thah

or for pleadin insanihy. I'll plead whahever ud takes to geh my freedom back. And don't tell me you'd do different if you were in my shoes.

ELAINE I'm as different to you as the auld world is from the new, sem as my father was. Oh, to be Joan of Arc goin up in a blaze to me maker.

FRANCES Then go up in a blaze to your maker, ony lave me alone. I've wan nigh here, wan night's freedom to mourn my daugher, to puh her in the clay tomorra beside her father.

ELAINE She's noh goin in wud him. My father's grave stays the way ud is. Can't ya just lave him alone?

FRANCES She's goin in beside him and thah's the end of ud, Elaine. Ud's whah he'd have wanted.

ELAINE Whah he'd have wanted?

BONIFACE Ud is, Elaine, ud's whah your father would've wanted.

ELAINE Whah my father wanted was to be above the ground, noh under ud. Above ud! You're noh shovellin her in on top of him. You stand here givin orders abouh hees grave. I organized hees burial. I picked the ploh, under the elms, near the path so he won't be too lonely. I paid for hees headstone. You weren't aven ah hees funeral.

FRANCES I wasn't fit to go, Elaine.

ELAINE But you're fit for Ariel's. You're ony here to swing the jury. Don't touch hees grave. Ud's mine. Ud's all ya've left me wud. I'm warnin ya now.

FRANCES Keep your grave. I've a new ploh arranged. Your father's moving, lock, stock and barrel as we spake. Ariel's goin in wud him. And I'll arrange the headstone this time. You think you can kick me when I'm down. I'm down, aye, righ now I'm lower than the lowest low. Buh I'll rise agin in spihe a your efforts to wipe the ground wud me. Why don't ya go and stay in the hotel tonigh, be asier for all of us. I'll be gone tomorra.

ELAINE I'm stayin here, to haunt ya.

FRANCES You? Haunt me? Oh, Elaine, you're ony the fallouh.

We never goh on, I don't know why I want us to
now. This skirmish betwane us is ancient. Y'ever
feel thah? Seems to me we been battlin a thousand
year.

ELAINE I'm goin down to hees grave and I hope for your
sake there's natin disturbed.

Exit ELAINE.

FRANCES Where did I geh her from?

She pours a drink.

BONIFACE (*Looking at* ARIEL *in coffin*) The divers found the
remains a seven people and they draggin the lake.
Wan wud a boulder tied round the skelehon of a
wrist. Most a them just an assortment a bones.
Found the skelehon of a pike too, massive, musta
been over two hundred pound, all the teeth intact.

FRANCES Did they find your mother?

BONIFACE We don't know yeh. They're tryin to date em all. I
tould em, she's the wan wud the boulder, but they
want to do their tests. (*To* ARIEL) I liked you, little
girl.

FRANCES (*To* STEPHEN) Shouldn't you be down ah the cement?

STEPHEN I was, cem home early because a the day is in ud.

FRANCES I been goin through the figures. Big losses these last
two months.

STEPHEN They don't listen to me.

FRANCES Make em listen. Tell em ud's comin down from me.
Ud's your inheritance.

STEPHEN I'll sell ud soon as ya sign ud over.

FRANCES Ya too much of a swank wud your film degree to
lower yourself to the cement and gravel.

STEPHEN I don't have me film degree yeh, thanks to certain
events round here.

FRANCES Well, mebbe ya should think abouh jackin in the
films and start turnin your mind to cement.

STEPHEN Thah's noh goin to happen, Ma.

FRANCES Me and your father built thah cement up from wan
lorry smuggled in from England, an auld shed and
the lase of a quarry. Cement built this house,
cement gev ya your education, your fast car, your
designer clothes, your foreign holidas. Cement
finances your arty films. You think you're above
the cement and gravel? Well, you're noh. You're
med of ud like the rest of us. Sure ya were nearly
born in wan a the lorries. Me and your father
drivin through the nigh, big delivery, me follyin
him along the weh roads. Elaine aslape beside me,
Ariel in front wud Fermoy. Me bapin like a
madwoman for Fermoy to pull over, him bapin
back thinkin I'm messin, and you surgin to be born.
I fling open the winda, wavin and yellin. He sees
me in the mirror and pulls over. Me in a panic, geh
me to the hospital, geh me to the midwives. Him
laughin ah me, I'll be your midwife, missus, and
the rain as balmy on him and the head of him
thrown back, laughin, just laughin . . . Was fierce
sorry after I didn't leh him be me midwife. He'd a
done ud too. Thah man was afraid a natin.

STEPHEN Ya boultin the stable now and your horse is gone.

FRANCES Doesn't everywan?

STEPHEN No, they don't, some knows when they're happy
ah the time. You had your chance, Ma, now ud's
mine, and I won't be buried under a ton a cement
on your whim. I tould ya I'd help ouh till the trial's
over. And I will. Buh then I'm gone.

FRANCES Is thah a threah?

STEPHEN Ud's a fact.

FRANCES Ya been listenin to Elaine. She's turnin ya against
me.

STEPHEN Can make up me own mind, Ma. Count yourself
lucky I can stand in the same room as ya.

FRANCES So that's the way ud is. I thought ya were on my side.

STEPHEN Ya though wrong. Ud's time ya stopped pullin ouh
a me, livin through me.

FRANCES I don't live through ya! How dare you! I've never

lived through anywan, to me own greah cost. Allas I've resisted. Allas! When ud'd be asier bow down. Whah are you sayin to me?

STEPHEN I'm sayin . . .

FRANCES All month long I been dramin I'm breastfeedin a snake. I thought ud was Elaine, buh ud's you. And insteada milk comin ouh ud's blood. And ya kape suckin though I'm roarin wud the pain. Ud took me ten year to wean you. Ten year I didn't have. And now you tell me thah doesn't count.

STEPHEN Ten year pretendin I was James. Ten year I went along wud ud. I used pray to die so you'd be given back James, I loved ya thah much. When strangers'd ask me me name, I'd say, James, me name is James, I'm James of the blue black curls.

FRANCES Whah are you talkin abouh, Stephen?

STEPHEN Don't pretend ya don't remember.

FRANCES I know I'd never win Mother a the Year, buh, Christ, Stephen, I wanted you as I wanted all me children. I swear, in me heart, what's left of ud, there's a tahhered chamber for each wan a ya. And them chambers is of equal measure.

STEPHEN And if they are, then why did ya kill my father?

FRANCES You know why.

STEPHEN Tell me.

FRANCES You know why, you know, because of her. (*Coffin*)

STEPHEN Wudouh a thought for Elaine or me. Wudouh a care of how thah rippin away has shahhered us. Ya did ud for Ariel. For James. There was ony ever two chambers in your heart, Ma, two dusty chambers, me and Elaine tryin to force our way in. Our playground was a graveyard, Ma, we ran among your tombstones like they were swings, we played hop, skip and jump on the bones a your children, your real children, while we whined for ya like ghosts. Isn't thah the way ud was? (*Gestures to coffin*) Isn't ud the way of ud still?

FRANCES Stephen . . . where a'ya goin?

STEPHEN (*Exiting*) The thing is, I'm goin.

She runs after him, tries to hold him back.

FRANCES   Ariel's funeral, me trial . . . Stephen! Don't, sweeheart, don't. Don't do this to me now. Please. Noh now. Noh now.

> STEPHEN *stands there, immovable.* FRANCES *withdraws eventually. Exit* STEPHEN. FRANCES *stands there distraught, disbelief.*

            (*Whispers*) He's gone . . . he's gone . . . my baby is gone.

BONIFACE   And leh him. Whah I shoulda done forty year ago. Good man, Stephen. How did ya do thah? Mammy's off the menu for ever more. Thah's how ud's done. Like thah big fah cluckin Mammy owl I seen on National Geographic the other nigh. And this Mammy Owl is huntin like Billy-O to fade Owl junior. And she comes back to the nest this nigh, big rah in her mouh, all important like, I'm fadin the young lad, aren't I a model Ma. And Junior's gone, fled when her back was turned, no goodbyes, thah's the way to do ud. Or salmon, sure salmon has ne'er a Ma ah all, and y'ever watch them, lords a the waher, sun shinin for em. Or trees, don't get me started on trees. Seems to me everythin worth lookin ah in this world has ne'er a Ma ah all, ud's just there be udself in a flowerin gorgeousness, orphaned and free.

FRANCES   Geh ouha my house, you.

BONIFACE   Whah?

FRANCES   You call yourself a man a God. Fermoy wud all hees divilry had more religion. Prancin around in your robes, watchin me like a hawk, cheerin on me ony son's departure.

BONIFACE   Frances, I was talkin abouh meself.

FRANCES   You knew all along and ya never said a word.

BONIFACE   Whah could I have done? I'm payin for this too.

FRANCES   Spare me your remorse. I rue the day I ever seh

eyes on the Fitzgeralds.

BONIFACE I think we can return the compliment.

FRANCES Just go.

BONIFACE I'm charged wud your care.

FRANCES The place is crawlin wud cops. I'm goin nowhere.
Just go. I want five minutes on me own wud Ariel.

BONIFACE I'll sih in the car. If ya nade anhin, I'll be in the car.

And exit BONIFACE. FRANCES *goes to coffin, looks in.*

FRANCES (*Whispers*) Mother a God, ya could be anywan.

Enter ELAINE, *stands there watching* FRANCES.

ELAINE So ya dug him up.

FRANCES Elaine, please, no more, no more, our love affair
wud the knife is over.

And exit FRANCES.

ELAINE (*To herself*) Alrigh. Lave her alone. Lave her alone.
Say natin. Do natin. She'll be gone tomorra and ya
can just dig him up agin. (*Wanders to coffin, looks in*)
Mebbe I'm unnatural buh I never fell under your
spell. Then the wrong things has allas moved me
. . . and if there's such a place as paradise, leh ud be
impty, oh leh ud be impty.

SARAH *has entered, listens.*

SARAH I've an inklin of whah you're plannin.

ELAINE I never plan anhin, Auntie Sarah.

SARAH Don't ya? (*Looks into coffin*) God, she's wizened to a
nuh. Wud a squaze ya'd fih her in a fishbowl.

ELAINE She's after diggin him up.

SARAH So? He was her husband, noh yours, and this is her
house, noh yours, and a body can do whah they like
behind their own front duur.

ELAINE Whah planet were you brough up on? Behind your

own front duur's the wan place ya can do natin ya like. Behind your own front duur's where ya face em all down wud your tail to the wall. And by God I'm goin to face thah wan down before long.

SARAH There's a divil the size of a whale inside you. Where in God's name is this hatred a your mother comin from?

ELAINE If I knew thah . . . I can't look ah her for too long or me head swims. She appals me, allas has. (*Shudders*) Her eyes, her shoulders, everythin abouh her. I look ah her and I think there's somethin missin. I don't know is ud in me or in her.

SARAH And whah is ud ya think is missin?

ELAINE I think she has no soul.

SARAH And since when have you become the decider a souls? A cuurse she has a soul, if she hadn't a soul she wouldn't be alive.

ELAINE They say there's some born wudouh em and I think she's wan a them. She tells me we been slashin wan another since time began. Well, if we have, this here is my turn, this is my opportunihy to geh a good go ah her and silence her till Judgement Day.

SARAH And on Judgement Day what'll ya tell the man above wud hees seven eyes level on ya? Ya won't face him down so aisy.

ELAINE You dare to talk to me abouh God and you the first thah coaxed the darkness in. I know you of an auld dahe. Addicted to nigh is what y'are, slobberin over ud like the cah wud the crame. But ya won't grab your own piece a nigh, no, ya covet mine from the corner. You ud was watched the first murder in this house. You watched your sister die, ya watched me grandfather tie her wud stones and ya said natin and ya done natin, ony watched in a swoon, black flowers sproutin ouha your chest. Yes, ya whispered, yes, I'll watch anhin, I'm the woman who'll watch anhin.

SARAH You don't know the first thing abouh me and me sister and your grandfather.

ELAINE I know ya married him.

SARAH Thah was the ind! Thah was the ind! I'm sick a bein judged on the ind. Whah abouh the start? Ya think I was never young? Ya think I like these auld hands, wud the veins risin on em like rivers in flood? Ya think I never burned? Ya think the world started wud you? I loved my sister. I adored thah woman.

ELAINE Aye, and ya adored her man wud your grady plain Jane heart. Oh aye, ya loved her alrigh, loved her so much ya wanted her life, her eyelashes, her children, her husband. And some goblin in me grandfather heard your prayers and answered em.

SARAH Ud was me he wint wud first. Me! Ya didn't know thah, did ya! And she took him from me wudouh a by your leave, wudouh an apology. And I took him back. Fair is fair.

ELAINE And you try to bate me over the head wud God, like you're hees favourihe, like you'll be sittin on hees knee on Judgement Day, wud me prostrahe before yees. God won't like me. I know thah. Buh he'll have more time for me than he will for you. You married your sister's husband as she turned to bog oak in Cuura Lake. Ya watched Ariel die, ya watched me father die. Is there anhin ya wouldn't watch?

SARAH To watch a thing is ony to half wish ud. And to half wish a thing is a long way off from doin ud. Buh I'll watch no longer. I'm bowin ouh here. I'm no match for ya anymore.

Exit SARAH.

ELAINE (*After her*) Good. Good. Good.

ELAINE *goes to coffin. Takes out skull of* ARIEL, *with a few strands of hair attached to it. She holds it up.*

(*To skull*) I drame abouh you all the time. Strange,

wakin there's no animosity, we're friends, friendly as sisters can be, buh aslape we're enemies, enemies till the end a time. Whah does thah mane? Remember them black dolls we had when we were scuts and how we used torture em on Sahurday mornins, line them up on the bed and tear em limb from limb? That's what ya remind me a now, them black dolls. Did ya go aisy, Ariel? Or did ya figh him ah the end? Or did ya think ud was all a game, smokin hees cigar and swillin hees brandy as the stars leant down to watch?

> FERMOY *stands in doorway, dressed as he was at end of Act Two. Covered in blood. He watches* ELAINE *dancing. She finally registers him, backs off.*

(*A whisper*) Daddy.
FERMOY (*Advancing*) Whah?
ELAINE Go way, keep away.
FERMOY Who are you?
ELAINE Ya don't know me.
FERMOY Don't I? I thought ya were familiar, walkin up the drive, the lawn, the fountain, thought I recognized this place from somewhere. Who are ya?
ELAINE Ya never give the dead your name.
FERMOY Am I dead?
ELAINE Oh, you're dead alrigh.
FERMOY Dead as thah? (*Points to skull*)
ELAINE Yeah.
FERMOY Who's thah?
ELAINE Me sister . . . Ariel . . . Ya remember her?
FERMOY Who?
ELAINE Ariel.
FERMOY No, should I?
ELAINE No.
FERMOY Then why did ya ask me?
ELAINE Never mind.
FERMOY Look, I'm tryin to find this place, ya may be able to help me.

ELAINE And whah place is ud you're tryin to find?

FERMOY I don't know the name of ud. (*Thinks*) Ud's a cuurtyard, yella, or the ligh in ud is yella. There's some
girl there I have to meeh. D'you know the place
I'm talkin abouh? Is ud anywhere 'round here?

ELAINE I never heard if ud is.

FERMOY Ya sure?

ELAINE Yeah.

FERMOY I have to get there . . . I have to meet this girl.
Nowan seems to know where ud is. I may kape
goin.

And exit FERMOY *as* FRANCES *enters.*

FRANCES Elaine.

Takes skull off ELAINE, *who looks after* FERMOY.

Just whah d'ya think you're doin . . . maulin her
like thah?

Puts skull back in coffin.

ELAINE I tould ya not to touch me father's grave. Tould
ya ih'd disturb everythin. But ya wouldn't listen,
would ya?

FRANCES Just geh ouh! Geh ouh a this house and don't come
back. You're so full a your own hate ya don't
nohice the hate of others. Some zebra stallion
grafted you onta me. I wanted a son to make up for
James. And I goh you. Now g'wan wud thah piece
of information and leh ud sustain ya on your
travels. G'wan, geh ouha me sigh.

ELAINE Aye, some zebra stallion grafted me onta ya alrigh,
and I festered there, bidin me time. Ya say ya
prayed for a son to make up for James. Well, I am
James. I'm James returned. And I'm me father that
ya butchered to hees eyeballs. And I'm Ariel. And
I'm Elaine wud your deah on me palm, carved inta

74

my plain a Mars like stone. Whah a relafe to be
finally livin ud.

Stabs FRANCES *in the throat.*

FRANCES (*Reels, falls*) Elaine . . . no . . . no . . . no more . . .
ELAINE (*Watching her reel, die, flounder*) After this, no more.
FRANCES No . . . (*Tries to get up, holds her throat, blood spilling
from her mouth*) Had to . . . had to . . . puh ud off . . .

*A massive effort to get up, gets up, holds onto coffin,
looks into it, a blood-curdling wail.*

No . . . no . . . Don't . . . don't leh me . . . don't leh me
. . . don't leh me . . . don't leh me go . . .

Falls against ELAINE *who lets her slide to the floor.*
ELAINE *stands there. Throws down the knife. Looks
out.*
'Mors et Vita' *music, and blackout.*

from 'The Vision of Hell' by Gustave Doré